C-3517   CAREER EXAMINATION SERIES

*This is your
PASSBOOK for...*

Administrative Space Analyst

*Test Preparation Study Guide
Questions & Answers*

COPYRIGHT NOTICE

This book is SOLELY intended for, is sold ONLY to, and its use is RESTRICTED to individual, bona fide applicants or candidates who qualify by virtue of having seriously filed applications for appropriate license, certificate, professional and/or promotional advancement, higher school matriculation, scholarship, or other legitimate requirements of education and/or governmental authorities.

This book is NOT intended for use, class instruction, tutoring, training, duplication, copying, reprinting, excerption, or adaptation, etc., by:

1) Other publishers
2) Proprietors and/or Instructors of "Coaching" and/or Preparatory Courses
3) Personnel and/or Training Divisions of commercial, industrial, and governmental organizations
4) Schools, colleges, or universities and/or their departments and staffs, including teachers and other personnel
5) Testing Agencies or Bureaus
6) Study groups which seek by the purchase of a single volume to copy and/or duplicate and/or adapt this material for use by the group as a whole without having purchased individual volumes for each of the members of the group
7) Et al.

Such persons would be in violation of appropriate Federal and State statutes.

PROVISION OF LICENSING AGREEMENTS – Recognized educational, commercial, industrial, and governmental institutions and organizations, and others legitimately engaged in educational pursuits, including training, testing, and measurement activities, may address request for a licensing agreement to the copyright owners, who will determine whether, and under what conditions, including fees and charges, the materials in this book may be used them. In other words, a licensing facility exists for the legitimate use of the material in this book on other than an individual basis. However, it is asseverated and affirmed here that the material in this book CANNOT be used without the receipt of the express permission of such a licensing agreement from the Publishers. Inquiries re licensing should be addressed to the company, attention rights and permissions department.

All rights reserved, including the right of reproduction in whole or in part, in any form or by any means, electronic or mechanical, including photocopying, recording, or by any information storage and retrieval system, without permission in writing from the Publisher.

Copyright © 2025 by
National Learning Corporation

212 Michael Drive, Syosset, NY 11791
(516) 921-8888 • www.passbooks.com
E-mail: info@passbooks.com

PASSBOOK® SERIES

THE *PASSBOOK® SERIES* has been created to prepare applicants and candidates for the ultimate academic battlefield – the examination room.

At some time in our lives, each and every one of us may be required to take an examination – for validation, matriculation, admission, qualification, registration, certification, or licensure.

Based on the assumption that every applicant or candidate has met the basic formal educational standards, has taken the required number of courses, and read the necessary texts, the *PASSBOOK® SERIES* furnishes the one special preparation which may assure passing with confidence, instead of failing with insecurity. Examination questions – together with answers – are furnished as the basic vehicle for study so that the mysteries of the examination and its compounding difficulties may be eliminated or diminished by a sure method.

This book is meant to help you pass your examination provided that you qualify and are serious in your objective.

The entire field is reviewed through the huge store of content information which is succinctly presented through a provocative and challenging approach – the question-and-answer method.

A climate of success is established by furnishing the correct answers at the end of each test.

You soon learn to recognize types of questions, forms of questions, and patterns of questioning. You may even begin to anticipate expected outcomes.

You perceive that many questions are repeated or adapted so that you can gain acute insights, which may enable you to score many sure points.

You learn how to confront new questions, or types of questions, and to attack them confidently and work out the correct answers.

You note objectives and emphases, and recognize pitfalls and dangers, so that you may make positive educational adjustments.

Moreover, you are kept fully informed in relation to new concepts, methods, practices, and directions in the field.

You discover that you are actually taking the examination all the time: you are preparing for the examination by "taking" an examination, not by reading extraneous and/or supererogatory textbooks.

In short, this PASSBOOK®, used directedly, should be an important factor in helping you to pass your test.

ADMINISTRATIVE SPACE ANALYST

JOB DESCRIPTION
With wide latitude for independent action, serves as space planning and utilization specialist and performs major duties relating to the regulation, study, survey, analysis, economic utilization and cancellation of city-owned and leased space; performs related work. Supervises Associate Space Analysts.

SCOPE OF THE EXAMINATION
The multiple-choice test may include questions on administration and supervisory principles and techniques including work scheduling, coordinating, planning and delegating; report writing; general building design and construction methods, techniques, and materials; Building Code, Fire Code and other related codes and safety standards; interior planning, space allocation standards; office procedures and requirements; measurement and space layout work related mathematics; standards of employee conduct; and other related areas.

HOW TO TAKE A TEST

I. YOU MUST PASS AN EXAMINATION

A. WHAT EVERY CANDIDATE SHOULD KNOW

Examination applicants often ask us for help in preparing for the written test. What can I study in advance? What kinds of questions will be asked? How will the test be given? How will the papers be graded?

As an applicant for a civil service examination, you may be wondering about some of these things. Our purpose here is to suggest effective methods of advance study and to describe civil service examinations.

Your chances for success on this examination can be increased if you know how to prepare. Those "pre-examination jitters" can be reduced if you know what to expect. You can even experience an adventure in good citizenship if you know why civil service exams are given.

B. WHY ARE CIVIL SERVICE EXAMINATIONS GIVEN?

Civil service examinations are important to you in two ways. As a citizen, you want public jobs filled by employees who know how to do their work. As a job seeker, you want a fair chance to compete for that job on an equal footing with other candidates. The best-known means of accomplishing this two-fold goal is the competitive examination.

Exams are widely publicized throughout the nation. They may be administered for jobs in federal, state, city, municipal, town or village governments or agencies.

Any citizen may apply, with some limitations, such as the age or residence of applicants. Your experience and education may be reviewed to see whether you meet the requirements for the particular examination. When these requirements exist, they are reasonable and applied consistently to all applicants. Thus, a competitive examination may cause you some uneasiness now, but it is your privilege and safeguard.

C. HOW ARE CIVIL SERVICE EXAMS DEVELOPED?

Examinations are carefully written by trained technicians who are specialists in the field known as "psychological measurement," in consultation with recognized authorities in the field of work that the test will cover. These experts recommend the subject matter areas or skills to be tested; only those knowledges or skills important to your success on the job are included. The most reliable books and source materials available are used as references. Together, the experts and technicians judge the difficulty level of the questions.

Test technicians know how to phrase questions so that the problem is clearly stated. Their ethics do not permit "trick" or "catch" questions. Questions may have been tried out on sample groups, or subjected to statistical analysis, to determine their usefulness.

Written tests are often used in combination with performance tests, ratings of training and experience, and oral interviews. All of these measures combine to form the best-known means of finding the right person for the right job.

II. HOW TO PASS THE WRITTEN TEST

A. NATURE OF THE EXAMINATION

To prepare intelligently for civil service examinations, you should know how they differ from school examinations you have taken. In school you were assigned certain definite pages to read or subjects to cover. The examination questions were quite detailed and usually emphasized memory. Civil service exams, on the other hand, try to discover your present ability to perform the duties of a position, plus your potentiality to learn these duties. In other words, a civil service exam attempts to predict how successful you will be. Questions cover such a broad area that they cannot be as minute and detailed as school exam questions.

In the public service similar kinds of work, or positions, are grouped together in one "class." This process is known as *position-classification*. All the positions in a class are paid according to the salary range for that class. One class title covers all of these positions, and they are all tested by the same examination.

B. FOUR BASIC STEPS

1) Study the announcement

How, then, can you know what subjects to study? Our best answer is: "Learn as much as possible about the class of positions for which you've applied." The exam will test the knowledge, skills and abilities needed to do the work.

Your most valuable source of information about the position you want is the official exam announcement. This announcement lists the training and experience qualifications. Check these standards and apply only if you come reasonably close to meeting them.

The brief description of the position in the examination announcement offers some clues to the subjects which will be tested. Think about the job itself. Review the duties in your mind. Can you perform them, or are there some in which you are rusty? Fill in the blank spots in your preparation.

Many jurisdictions preview the written test in the exam announcement by including a section called "Knowledge and Abilities Required," "Scope of the Examination," or some similar heading. Here you will find out specifically what fields will be tested.

2) Review your own background

Once you learn in general what the position is all about, and what you need to know to do the work, ask yourself which subjects you already know fairly well and which need improvement. You may wonder whether to concentrate on improving your strong areas or on building some background in your fields of weakness. When the announcement has specified "some knowledge" or "considerable knowledge," or has used adjectives like "beginning principles of..." or "advanced ... methods," you can get a clue as to the number and difficulty of questions to be asked in any given field. More questions, and hence broader coverage, would be included for those subjects which are more important in the work. Now weigh your strengths and weaknesses against the job requirements and prepare accordingly.

3) Determine the level of the position

Another way to tell how intensively you should prepare is to understand the level of the job for which you are applying. Is it the entering level? In other words, is this the position in which beginners in a field of work are hired? Or is it an intermediate or advanced level? Sometimes this is indicated by such words as "Junior" or "Senior" in the class title. Other jurisdictions use Roman numerals to designate the level – Clerk I, Clerk II, for example. The word "Supervisor" sometimes appears in the title. If the level is not indicated by the title, check the description of duties. Will you be working under very close supervision, or will you have responsibility for independent decisions in this work?

4) Choose appropriate study materials

Now that you know the subjects to be examined and the relative amount of each subject to be covered, you can choose suitable study materials. For beginning level jobs, or even advanced ones, if you have a pronounced weakness in some aspect of your training, read a modern, standard textbook in that field. Be sure it is up to date and has general coverage. Such books are normally available at your library, and the librarian will be glad to help you locate one. For entry-level positions, questions of appropriate difficulty are chosen – neither highly advanced questions, nor those too simple. Such questions require careful thought but not advanced training.

If the position for which you are applying is technical or advanced, you will read more advanced, specialized material. If you are already familiar with the basic principles of your field, elementary textbooks would waste your time. Concentrate on advanced textbooks and technical periodicals. Think through the concepts and review difficult problems in your field.

These are all general sources. You can get more ideas on your own initiative, following these leads. For example, training manuals and publications of the government agency which employs workers in your field can be useful, particularly for technical and professional positions. A letter or visit to the government department involved may result in more specific study suggestions, and certainly will provide you with a more definite idea of the exact nature of the position you are seeking.

III. KINDS OF TESTS

Tests are used for purposes other than measuring knowledge and ability to perform specified duties. For some positions, it is equally important to test ability to make adjustments to new situations or to profit from training. In others, basic mental abilities not dependent on information are essential. Questions which test these things may not appear as pertinent to the duties of the position as those which test for knowledge and information. Yet they are often highly important parts of a fair examination. For very general questions, it is almost impossible to help you direct your study efforts. What we can do is to point out some of the more common of these general abilities needed in public service positions and describe some typical questions.

1) General information

Broad, general information has been found useful for predicting job success in some kinds of work. This is tested in a variety of ways, from vocabulary lists to questions about current events. Basic background in some field of work, such as sociology or economics, may be sampled in a group of questions. Often these are principles which have become familiar to most persons through exposure rather than through formal training. It is difficult to advise you how to study for these questions; being alert to the world around you is our best suggestion.

2) Verbal ability

An example of an ability needed in many positions is verbal or language ability. Verbal ability is, in brief, the ability to use and understand words. Vocabulary and grammar tests are typical measures of this ability. Reading comprehension or paragraph interpretation questions are common in many kinds of civil service tests. You are given a paragraph of written material and asked to find its central meaning.

3) Numerical ability

Number skills can be tested by the familiar arithmetic problem, by checking paired lists of numbers to see which are alike and which are different, or by interpreting charts and graphs. In the latter test, a graph may be printed in the test booklet which you are asked to use as the basis for answering questions.

4) Observation

A popular test for law-enforcement positions is the observation test. A picture is shown to you for several minutes, then taken away. Questions about the picture test your ability to observe both details and larger elements.

5) Following directions

In many positions in the public service, the employee must be able to carry out written instructions dependably and accurately. You may be given a chart with several columns, each column listing a variety of information. The questions require you to carry out directions involving the information given in the chart.

6) Skills and aptitudes

Performance tests effectively measure some manual skills and aptitudes. When the skill is one in which you are trained, such as typing or shorthand, you can practice. These tests are often very much like those given in business school or high school courses. For many of the other skills and aptitudes, however, no short-time preparation can be made. Skills and abilities natural to you or that you have developed throughout your lifetime are being tested.

Many of the general questions just described provide all the data needed to answer the questions and ask you to use your reasoning ability to find the answers. Your best preparation for these tests, as well as for tests of facts and ideas, is to be at your physical and mental best. You, no doubt, have your own methods of getting into an exam-taking mood and keeping "in shape." The next section lists some ideas on this subject.

IV. KINDS OF QUESTIONS

Only rarely is the "essay" question, which you answer in narrative form, used in civil service tests. Civil service tests are usually of the short-answer type. Full instructions for answering these questions will be given to you at the examination. But in case this is your first experience with short-answer questions and separate answer sheets, here is what you need to know:

1) **Multiple-choice Questions**

Most popular of the short-answer questions is the "multiple choice" or "best answer" question. It can be used, for example, to test for factual knowledge, ability to solve problems or judgment in meeting situations found at work.

A multiple-choice question is normally one of three types—
- It can begin with an incomplete statement followed by several possible endings. You are to find the one ending which *best* completes the statement, although some of the others may not be entirely wrong.
- It can also be a complete statement in the form of a question which is answered by choosing one of the statements listed.

- It can be in the form of a problem – again you select the best answer.

Here is an example of a multiple-choice question with a discussion which should give you some clues as to the method for choosing the right answer:

When an employee has a complaint about his assignment, the action which will *best* help him overcome his difficulty is to
   A. discuss his difficulty with his coworkers
   B. take the problem to the head of the organization
   C. take the problem to the person who gave him the assignment
   D. say nothing to anyone about his complaint

In answering this question, you should study each of the choices to find which is best. Consider choice "A" – Certainly an employee may discuss his complaint with fellow employees, but no change or improvement can result, and the complaint remains unresolved. Choice "B" is a poor choice since the head of the organization probably does not know what assignment you have been given, and taking your problem to him is known as "going over the head" of the supervisor. The supervisor, or person who made the assignment, is the person who can clarify it or correct any injustice. Choice "C" is, therefore, correct. To say nothing, as in choice "D," is unwise. Supervisors have and interest in knowing the problems employees are facing, and the employee is seeking a solution to his problem.

2) True/False Questions

The "true/false" or "right/wrong" form of question is sometimes used. Here a complete statement is given. Your job is to decide whether the statement is right or wrong.

SAMPLE: A roaming cell-phone call to a nearby city costs less than a non-roaming call to a distant city.

This statement is wrong, or false, since roaming calls are more expensive.

This is not a complete list of all possible question forms, although most of the others are variations of these common types. You will always get complete directions for answering questions. Be sure you understand *how* to mark your answers – ask questions until you do.

V. RECORDING YOUR ANSWERS

Computer terminals are used more and more today for many different kinds of exams.
For an examination with very few applicants, you may be told to record your answers in the test booklet itself. Separate answer sheets are much more common. If this separate answer sheet is to be scored by machine – and this is often the case – it is highly important that you mark your answers correctly in order to get credit.
An electronic scoring machine is often used in civil service offices because of the speed with which papers can be scored. Machine-scored answer sheets must be marked with a pencil, which will be given to you. This pencil has a high graphite content which responds to the electronic scoring machine. As a matter of fact, stray dots may register as answers, so do not let your pencil rest on the answer sheet while you are pondering the correct answer. Also, if your pencil lead breaks or is otherwise defective, ask for another.

Since the answer sheet will be dropped in a slot in the scoring machine, be careful not to bend the corners or get the paper crumpled.

The answer sheet normally has five vertical columns of numbers, with 30 numbers to a column. These numbers correspond to the question numbers in your test booklet. After each number, going across the page are four or five pairs of dotted lines. These short dotted lines have small letters or numbers above them. The first two pairs may also have a "T" or "F" above the letters. This indicates that the first two pairs only are to be used if the questions are of the true-false type. If the questions are multiple choice, disregard the "T" and "F" and pay attention only to the small letters or numbers.

Answer your questions in the manner of the sample that follows:

32. The largest city in the United States is
    A. Washington, D.C.
    B. New York City
    C. Chicago
    D. Detroit
    E. San Francisco

1) Choose the answer you think is best. (New York City is the largest, so "B" is correct.)
2) Find the row of dotted lines numbered the same as the question you are answering. (Find row number 32)
3) Find the pair of dotted lines corresponding to the answer. (Find the pair of lines under the mark "B.")
4) Make a solid black mark between the dotted lines.

VI. BEFORE THE TEST

Common sense will help you find procedures to follow to get ready for an examination. Too many of us, however, overlook these sensible measures. Indeed, nervousness and fatigue have been found to be the most serious reasons why applicants fail to do their best on civil service tests. Here is a list of reminders:

- Begin your preparation early – Don't wait until the last minute to go scurrying around for books and materials or to find out what the position is all about.
- Prepare continuously – An hour a night for a week is better than an all-night cram session. This has been definitely established. What is more, a night a week for a month will return better dividends than crowding your study into a shorter period of time.
- Locate the place of the exam – You have been sent a notice telling you when and where to report for the examination. If the location is in a different town or otherwise unfamiliar to you, it would be well to inquire the best route and learn something about the building.
- Relax the night before the test – Allow your mind to rest. Do not study at all that night. Plan some mild recreation or diversion; then go to bed early and get a good night's sleep.
- Get up early enough to make a leisurely trip to the place for the test – This way unforeseen events, traffic snarls, unfamiliar buildings, etc. will not upset you.
- Dress comfortably – A written test is not a fashion show. You will be known by number and not by name, so wear something comfortable.

- Leave excess paraphernalia at home – Shopping bags and odd bundles will get in your way. You need bring only the items mentioned in the official notice you received; usually everything you need is provided. Do not bring reference books to the exam. They will only confuse those last minutes and be taken away from you when in the test room.
- Arrive somewhat ahead of time – If because of transportation schedules you must get there very early, bring a newspaper or magazine to take your mind off yourself while waiting.
- Locate the examination room – When you have found the proper room, you will be directed to the seat or part of the room where you will sit. Sometimes you are given a sheet of instructions to read while you are waiting. Do not fill out any forms until you are told to do so; just read them and be prepared.
- Relax and prepare to listen to the instructions
- If you have any physical problem that may keep you from doing your best, be sure to tell the test administrator. If you are sick or in poor health, you really cannot do your best on the exam. You can come back and take the test some other time.

VII. AT THE TEST

The day of the test is here and you have the test booklet in your hand. The temptation to get going is very strong. Caution! There is more to success than knowing the right answers. You must know how to identify your papers and understand variations in the type of short-answer question used in this particular examination. Follow these suggestions for maximum results from your efforts:

1) Cooperate with the monitor

The test administrator has a duty to create a situation in which you can be as much at ease as possible. He will give instructions, tell you when to begin, check to see that you are marking your answer sheet correctly, and so on. He is not there to guard you, although he will see that your competitors do not take unfair advantage. He wants to help you do your best.

2) Listen to all instructions

Don't jump the gun! Wait until you understand all directions. In most civil service tests you get more time than you need to answer the questions. So don't be in a hurry. Read each word of instructions until you clearly understand the meaning. Study the examples, listen to all announcements and follow directions. Ask questions if you do not understand what to do.

3) Identify your papers

Civil service exams are usually identified by number only. You will be assigned a number; you must not put your name on your test papers. Be sure to copy your number correctly. Since more than one exam may be given, copy your exact examination title.

4) Plan your time

Unless you are told that a test is a "speed" or "rate of work" test, speed itself is usually not important. Time enough to answer all the questions will be provided, but this does not mean that you have all day. An overall time limit has been set. Divide the total time (in minutes) by the number of questions to determine the approximate time you have for each question.

5) Do not linger over difficult questions

If you come across a difficult question, mark it with a paper clip (useful to have along) and come back to it when you have been through the booklet. One caution if you do this – be sure to skip a number on your answer sheet as well. Check often to be sure that you have not lost your place and that you are marking in the row numbered the same as the question you are answering.

6) Read the questions

Be sure you know what the question asks! Many capable people are unsuccessful because they failed to *read* the questions correctly.

7) Answer all questions

Unless you have been instructed that a penalty will be deducted for incorrect answers, it is better to guess than to omit a question.

8) Speed tests

It is often better NOT to guess on speed tests. It has been found that on timed tests people are tempted to spend the last few seconds before time is called in marking answers at random – without even reading them – in the hope of picking up a few extra points. To discourage this practice, the instructions may warn you that your score will be "corrected" for guessing. That is, a penalty will be applied. The incorrect answers will be deducted from the correct ones, or some other penalty formula will be used.

9) Review your answers

If you finish before time is called, go back to the questions you guessed or omitted to give them further thought. Review other answers if you have time.

10) Return your test materials

If you are ready to leave before others have finished or time is called, take ALL your materials to the monitor and leave quietly. Never take any test material with you. The monitor can discover whose papers are not complete, and taking a test booklet may be grounds for disqualification.

VIII. EXAMINATION TECHNIQUES

1) Read the general instructions carefully. These are usually printed on the first page of the exam booklet. As a rule, these instructions refer to the timing of the examination; the fact that you should not start work until the signal and must stop work at a signal, etc. If there are any *special* instructions, such as a choice of questions to be answered, make sure that you note this instruction carefully.

2) When you are ready to start work on the examination, that is as soon as the signal has been given, read the instructions to each question booklet, underline any key words or phrases, such as *least, best, outline, describe* and the like. In this way you will tend to answer as requested rather than discover on reviewing your paper that you *listed without describing*, that you selected the *worst* choice rather than the *best* choice, etc.

3) If the examination is of the objective or multiple-choice type – that is, each question will also give a series of possible answers: A, B, C or D, and you are called upon to select the best answer and write the letter next to that answer on your answer paper – it is advisable to start answering each question in turn. There may be anywhere from 50 to 100 such questions in the three or four hours allotted and you can see how much time would be taken if you read through all the questions before beginning to answer any. Furthermore, if you come across a question or group of questions which you know would be difficult to answer, it would undoubtedly affect your handling of all the other questions.

4) If the examination is of the essay type and contains but a few questions, it is a moot point as to whether you should read all the questions before starting to answer any one. Of course, if you are given a choice – say five out of seven and the like – then it is essential to read all the questions so you can eliminate the two that are most difficult. If, however, you are asked to answer all the questions, there may be danger in trying to answer the easiest one first because you may find that you will spend too much time on it. The best technique is to answer the first question, then proceed to the second, etc.

5) Time your answers. Before the exam begins, write down the time it started, then add the time allowed for the examination and write down the time it must be completed, then divide the time available somewhat as follows:
    - If 3-1/2 hours are allowed, that would be 210 minutes. If you have 80 objective-type questions, that would be an average of 2-1/2 minutes per question. Allow yourself no more than 2 minutes per question, or a total of 160 minutes, which will permit about 50 minutes to review.
    - If for the time allotment of 210 minutes there are 7 essay questions to answer, that would average about 30 minutes a question. Give yourself only 25 minutes per question so that you have about 35 minutes to review.

6) The most important instruction is to *read each question* and make sure you know what is wanted. The second most important instruction is to *time yourself properly* so that you answer every question. The third most important instruction is to *answer every question*. Guess if you have to but include something for each question. Remember that you will receive no credit for a blank and will probably receive some credit if you write something in answer to an essay question. If you guess a letter – say "B" for a multiple-choice question – you may have guessed right. If you leave a blank as an answer to a multiple-choice question, the examiners may respect your feelings but it will not add a point to your score. Some exams may penalize you for wrong answers, so in such cases *only*, you may not want to guess unless you have some basis for your answer.

7) Suggestions
    a. Objective-type questions
        1. Examine the question booklet for proper sequence of pages and questions
        2. Read all instructions carefully
        3. Skip any question which seems too difficult; return to it after all other questions have been answered
        4. Apportion your time properly; do not spend too much time on any single question or group of questions

5. Note and underline key words – *all, most, fewest, least, best, worst, same, opposite,* etc.
6. Pay particular attention to negatives
7. Note unusual option, e.g., unduly long, short, complex, different or similar in content to the body of the question
8. Observe the use of "hedging" words – *probably, may, most likely,* etc.
9. Make sure that your answer is put next to the same number as the question
10. Do not second-guess unless you have good reason to believe the second answer is definitely more correct
11. Cross out original answer if you decide another answer is more accurate; do not erase until you are ready to hand your paper in
12. Answer all questions; guess unless instructed otherwise
13. Leave time for review

   b. Essay questions
1. Read each question carefully
2. Determine exactly what is wanted. Underline key words or phrases.
3. Decide on outline or paragraph answer
4. Include many different points and elements unless asked to develop any one or two points or elements
5. Show impartiality by giving pros and cons unless directed to select one side only
6. Make and write down any assumptions you find necessary to answer the questions
7. Watch your English, grammar, punctuation and choice of words
8. Time your answers; don't crowd material

8) Answering the essay question

Most essay questions can be answered by framing the specific response around several key words or ideas. Here are a few such key words or ideas:

M's: manpower, materials, methods, money, management
P's: purpose, program, policy, plan, procedure, practice, problems, pitfalls, personnel, public relations

   a. Six basic steps in handling problems:
1. Preliminary plan and background development
2. Collect information, data and facts
3. Analyze and interpret information, data and facts
4. Analyze and develop solutions as well as make recommendations
5. Prepare report and sell recommendations
6. Install recommendations and follow up effectiveness

   b. Pitfalls to avoid
1. *Taking things for granted* – A statement of the situation does not necessarily imply that each of the elements is necessarily true; for example, a complaint may be invalid and biased so that all that can be taken for granted is that a complaint has been registered

2. *Considering only one side of a situation* – Wherever possible, indicate several alternatives and then point out the reasons you selected the best one
3. *Failing to indicate follow up* – Whenever your answer indicates action on your part, make certain that you will take proper follow-up action to see how successful your recommendations, procedures or actions turn out to be
4. *Taking too long in answering any single question* – Remember to time your answers properly

IX. AFTER THE TEST

Scoring procedures differ in detail among civil service jurisdictions although the general principles are the same. Whether the papers are hand-scored or graded by machine we have described, they are nearly always graded by number. That is, the person who marks the paper knows only the number – never the name – of the applicant. Not until all the papers have been graded will they be matched with names. If other tests, such as training and experience or oral interview ratings have been given, scores will be combined. Different parts of the examination usually have different weights. For example, the written test might count 60 percent of the final grade, and a rating of training and experience 40 percent. In many jurisdictions, veterans will have a certain number of points added to their grades.

After the final grade has been determined, the names are placed in grade order and an eligible list is established. There are various methods for resolving ties between those who get the same final grade – probably the most common is to place first the name of the person whose application was received first. Job offers are made from the eligible list in the order the names appear on it. You will be notified of your grade and your rank as soon as all these computations have been made. This will be done as rapidly as possible.

People who are found to meet the requirements in the announcement are called "eligibles." Their names are put on a list of eligible candidates. An eligible's chances of getting a job depend on how high he stands on this list and how fast agencies are filling jobs from the list.

When a job is to be filled from a list of eligibles, the agency asks for the names of people on the list of eligibles for that job. When the civil service commission receives this request, it sends to the agency the names of the three people highest on this list. Or, if the job to be filled has specialized requirements, the office sends the agency the names of the top three persons who meet these requirements from the general list.

The appointing officer makes a choice from among the three people whose names were sent to him. If the selected person accepts the appointment, the names of the others are put back on the list to be considered for future openings.

That is the rule in hiring from all kinds of eligible lists, whether they are for typist, carpenter, chemist, or something else. For every vacancy, the appointing officer has his choice of any one of the top three eligibles on the list. This explains why the person whose name is on top of the list sometimes does not get an appointment when some of the persons lower on the list do. If the appointing officer chooses the second or third eligible, the No. 1 eligible does not get a job at once, but stays on the list until he is appointed or the list is terminated.

X. HOW TO PASS THE INTERVIEW TEST

The examination for which you applied requires an oral interview test. You have already taken the written test and you are now being called for the interview test – the final part of the formal examination.

You may think that it is not possible to prepare for an interview test and that there are no procedures to follow during an interview. Our purpose is to point out some things you can do in advance that will help you and some good rules to follow and pitfalls to avoid while you are being interviewed.

What is an interview supposed to test?

The written examination is designed to test the technical knowledge and competence of the candidate; the oral is designed to evaluate intangible qualities, not readily measured otherwise, and to establish a list showing the relative fitness of each candidate – as measured against his competitors – for the position sought. Scoring is not on the basis of "right" and "wrong," but on a sliding scale of values ranging from "not passable" to "outstanding." As a matter of fact, it is possible to achieve a relatively low score without a single "incorrect" answer because of evident weakness in the qualities being measured.

Occasionally, an examination may consist entirely of an oral test – either an individual or a group oral. In such cases, information is sought concerning the technical knowledges and abilities of the candidate, since there has been no written examination for this purpose. More commonly, however, an oral test is used to supplement a written examination.

Who conducts interviews?

The composition of oral boards varies among different jurisdictions. In nearly all, a representative of the personnel department serves as chairman. One of the members of the board may be a representative of the department in which the candidate would work. In some cases, "outside experts" are used, and, frequently, a businessman or some other representative of the general public is asked to serve. Labor and management or other special groups may be represented. The aim is to secure the services of experts in the appropriate field.

However the board is composed, it is a good idea (and not at all improper or unethical) to ascertain in advance of the interview who the members are and what groups they represent. When you are introduced to them, you will have some idea of their backgrounds and interests, and at least you will not stutter and stammer over their names.

What should be done before the interview?

While knowledge about the board members is useful and takes some of the surprise element out of the interview, there is other preparation which is more substantive. It *is* possible to prepare for an oral interview – in several ways:

1) Keep a copy of your application and review it carefully before the interview

This may be the only document before the oral board, and the starting point of the interview. Know what education and experience you have listed there, and the sequence and dates of all of it. Sometimes the board will ask you to review the highlights of your experience for them; you should not have to hem and haw doing it.

2) Study the class specification and the examination announcement

Usually, the oral board has one or both of these to guide them. The qualities, characteristics or knowledges required by the position sought are stated in these documents. They offer valuable clues as to the nature of the oral interview. For example, if the job involves supervisory responsibilities, the announcement will usually indicate that knowledge of modern supervisory methods and the qualifications of the candidate as a supervisor will be tested. If so, you can expect such questions, frequently in the form of a hypothetical situation which you are expected to solve. NEVER go into an oral without knowledge of the duties and responsibilities of the job you seek.

3) Think through each qualification required

Try to visualize the kind of questions you would ask if you were a board member. How well could you answer them? Try especially to appraise your own knowledge and background in each area, *measured against the job sought*, and identify any areas in which you are weak. Be critical and realistic – do not flatter yourself.

4) Do some general reading in areas in which you feel you may be weak

For example, if the job involves supervision and your past experience has NOT, some general reading in supervisory methods and practices, particularly in the field of human relations, might be useful. Do NOT study agency procedures or detailed manuals. The oral board will be testing your understanding and capacity, not your memory.

5) Get a good night's sleep and watch your general health and mental attitude

You will want a clear head at the interview. Take care of a cold or any other minor ailment, and of course, no hangovers.

What should be done on the day of the interview?

Now comes the day of the interview itself. Give yourself plenty of time to get there. Plan to arrive somewhat ahead of the scheduled time, particularly if your appointment is in the fore part of the day. If a previous candidate fails to appear, the board might be ready for you a bit early. By early afternoon an oral board is almost invariably behind schedule if there are many candidates, and you may have to wait. Take along a book or magazine to read, or your application to review, but leave any extraneous material in the waiting room when you go in for your interview. In any event, relax and compose yourself.

The matter of dress is important. The board is forming impressions about you – from your experience, your manners, your attitude, and your appearance. Give your personal appearance careful attention. Dress your best, but not your flashiest. Choose conservative, appropriate clothing, and be sure it is immaculate. This is a business interview, and your appearance should indicate that you regard it as such. Besides, being well groomed and properly dressed will help boost your confidence.

Sooner or later, someone will call your name and escort you into the interview room. *This is it.* From here on you are on your own. It is too late for any more preparation. But remember, you asked for this opportunity to prove your fitness, and you are here because your request was granted.

What happens when you go in?

The usual sequence of events will be as follows: The clerk (who is often the board stenographer) will introduce you to the chairman of the oral board, who will introduce you to the other members of the board. Acknowledge the introductions before you sit down. Do not be surprised if you find a microphone facing you or a stenotypist sitting by. Oral interviews are usually recorded in the event of an appeal or other review.

Usually the chairman of the board will open the interview by reviewing the highlights of your education and work experience from your application – primarily for the benefit of the other members of the board, as well as to get the material into the record. Do not interrupt or comment unless there is an error or significant misinterpretation; if that is the case, do not hesitate. But do not quibble about insignificant matters. Also, he will usually ask you some question about your education, experience or your present job – partly to get you to start talking and to establish the interviewing "rapport." He may start the actual questioning, or turn it over to one of the other members. Frequently, each member undertakes the questioning on a particular area, one in which he is perhaps most competent, so you can expect each member to participate in the examination. Because time is limited, you may also expect some rather abrupt switches in the direction the questioning takes, so do not be upset by it. Normally, a board member will not pursue a single line of questioning unless he discovers a particular strength or weakness.

After each member has participated, the chairman will usually ask whether any member has any further questions, then will ask you if you have anything you wish to add. Unless you are expecting this question, it may floor you. Worse, it may start you off on an extended, extemporaneous speech. The board is not usually seeking more information. The question is principally to offer you a last opportunity to present further qualifications or to indicate that you have nothing to add. So, if you feel that a significant qualification or characteristic has been overlooked, it is proper to point it out in a sentence or so. Do not compliment the board on the thoroughness of their examination – they have been sketchy, and you know it. If you wish, merely say, "No thank you, I have nothing further to add." This is a point where you can "talk yourself out" of a good impression or fail to present an important bit of information. Remember, *you close the interview yourself*.

The chairman will then say, "That is all, Mr. _____, thank you." Do not be startled; the interview is over, and quicker than you think. Thank him, gather your belongings and take your leave. Save your sigh of relief for the other side of the door.

How to put your best foot forward

Throughout this entire process, you may feel that the board individually and collectively is trying to pierce your defenses, seek out your hidden weaknesses and embarrass and confuse you. Actually, this is not true. They are obliged to make an appraisal of your qualifications for the job you are seeking, and they want to see you in your best light. Remember, they must interview all candidates and a non-cooperative candidate may become a failure in spite of their best efforts to bring out his qualifications. Here are 15 suggestions that will help you:

1) Be natural – Keep your attitude confident, not cocky

If you are not confident that you can do the job, do not expect the board to be. Do not apologize for your weaknesses, try to bring out your strong points. The board is interested in a positive, not negative, presentation. Cockiness will antagonize any board member and make him wonder if you are covering up a weakness by a false show of strength.

2) Get comfortable, but don't lounge or sprawl

Sit erectly but not stiffly. A careless posture may lead the board to conclude that you are careless in other things, or at least that you are not impressed by the importance of the occasion. Either conclusion is natural, even if incorrect. Do not fuss with your clothing, a pencil or an ashtray. Your hands may occasionally be useful to emphasize a point; do not let them become a point of distraction.

3) Do not wisecrack or make small talk

This is a serious situation, and your attitude should show that you consider it as such. Further, the time of the board is limited – they do not want to waste it, and neither should you.

4) Do not exaggerate your experience or abilities

In the first place, from information in the application or other interviews and sources, the board may know more about you than you think. Secondly, you probably will not get away with it. An experienced board is rather adept at spotting such a situation, so do not take the chance.

5) If you know a board member, do not make a point of it, yet do not hide it

Certainly you are not fooling him, and probably not the other members of the board. Do not try to take advantage of your acquaintanceship – it will probably do you little good.

6) Do not dominate the interview

Let the board do that. They will give you the clues – do not assume that you have to do all the talking. Realize that the board has a number of questions to ask you, and do not try to take up all the interview time by showing off your extensive knowledge of the answer to the first one.

7) Be attentive

You only have 20 minutes or so, and you should keep your attention at its sharpest throughout. When a member is addressing a problem or question to you, give him your undivided attention. Address your reply principally to him, but do not exclude the other board members.

8) Do not interrupt

A board member may be stating a problem for you to analyze. He will ask you a question when the time comes. Let him state the problem, and wait for the question.

9) Make sure you understand the question

Do not try to answer until you are sure what the question is. If it is not clear, restate it in your own words or ask the board member to clarify it for you. However, do not haggle about minor elements.

10) Reply promptly but not hastily

A common entry on oral board rating sheets is "candidate responded readily," or "candidate hesitated in replies." Respond as promptly and quickly as you can, but do not jump to a hasty, ill-considered answer.

11) Do not be peremptory in your answers

A brief answer is proper – but do not fire your answer back. That is a losing game from your point of view. The board member can probably ask questions much faster than you can answer them.

12) Do not try to create the answer you think the board member wants

He is interested in what kind of mind you have and how it works – not in playing games. Furthermore, he can usually spot this practice and will actually grade you down on it.

13) Do not switch sides in your reply merely to agree with a board member

Frequently, a member will take a contrary position merely to draw you out and to see if you are willing and able to defend your point of view. Do not start a debate, yet do not surrender a good position. If a position is worth taking, it is worth defending.

14) Do not be afraid to admit an error in judgment if you are shown to be wrong

The board knows that you are forced to reply without any opportunity for careful consideration. Your answer may be demonstrably wrong. If so, admit it and get on with the interview.

15) Do not dwell at length on your present job

The opening question may relate to your present assignment. Answer the question but do not go into an extended discussion. You are being examined for a *new* job, not your present one. As a matter of fact, try to phrase ALL your answers in terms of the job for which you are being examined.

Basis of Rating

Probably you will forget most of these "do's" and "don'ts" when you walk into the oral interview room. Even remembering them all will not ensure you a passing grade. Perhaps you did not have the qualifications in the first place. But remembering them will help you to put your best foot forward, without treading on the toes of the board members.

Rumor and popular opinion to the contrary notwithstanding, an oral board wants you to make the best appearance possible. They know you are under pressure – but they also want to see how you respond to it as a guide to what your reaction would be under the pressures of the job you seek. They will be influenced by the degree of poise you display, the personal traits you show and the manner in which you respond.

ABOUT THIS BOOK

This book contains tests divided into Examination Sections. Go through each test, answering every question in the margin. We have also attached a sample answer sheet at the back of the book that can be removed and used. At the end of each test look at the answer key and check your answers. On the ones you got wrong, look at the right answer choice and learn. Do not fill in the answers first. Do not memorize the questions and answers, but understand the answer and principles involved. On your test, the questions will likely be different from the samples. Questions are changed and new ones added. If you understand these past questions you should have success with any changes that arise. Tests may consist of several types of questions. We have additional books on each subject should more study be advisable or necessary for you. Finally, the more you study, the better prepared you will be. This book is intended to be the last thing you study before you walk into the examination room. Prior study of relevant texts is also recommended. NLC publishes some of these in our Fundamental Series. Knowledge and good sense are important factors in passing your exam. Good luck also helps. So now study this Passbook, absorb the material contained within and take that knowledge into the examination. Then do your best to pass that exam.

EXAMINATION SECTION

EXAMINATION SECTION
TEST 1

DIRECTIONS: Each question or incomplete statement is followed by several suggested answers or completions. Select the one that BEST answers the question or completes the statement. *PRINT THE LETTER OF THE CORRECT ANSWER IN THE SPACE AT THE RIGHT*

1. Of the following, the BEST statement concerning the placement of *Conclusions and Recommendations* in a management report is:

    A. Recommendations should always be included in a report unless the report presents the results of an investigation
    B. If a report presents conclusions, it must present recommendations
    C. Every statement that is a conclusion should grow out of facts given elsewhere in the report
    D. Conclusions and recommendations should always conclude the report because they depend on its contents

2. Assume you are preparing a systematic analysis of your agency's pest control program and its effect on eliminating rodent infestation of premises in a specific region.
   To omit from your report important facts which you originally received from the person to whom you are reporting is GENERALLY considered to be

    A. *desirable;* anyone who is likely to read the report can consult his files for extra information
    B. *undesirable;* the report should include major facts that are obtained as a result of your efforts
    C. *desirable;* the person you are reporting to does not
    D. pass the report on to others who lack his own familiarity with the subject
    E. *undesirable;* the report should include all of the facts that are obtained as a result of your efforts

3. Of all the nonverbal devices used in report writing, tables are used most frequently to enable a reader to compare statistical information more easily. Hence, it is important that an analyst know when to use tables.
   Which one of the following statements that relate to tables is generally considered to be LEAST valid?

    A. A table from an outside source must be acknowledged by the report writer.
    B. A table should be placed far in advance of the point where it is referred to or discussed in the report.
    C. The notes applying to a table are placed at the bottom of the table, rather than at the bottom of the page on which the table is found.
    D. A table should indicate the major factors that effect the data it contains.

4. Assume that an analyst writes reports which contain more detail than might be needed to serve their purpose.
   Such a practice is GENERALLY considered to be

A. *desirable;* this additional detail permits maximized machine utilization
B. *undesirable;* if specifications of reports are defined when they are first set up, loss of flexibility will follow
C. *desirable;* everything ought to be recorded so it will be there if it is ever needed
D. *undesirable;* recipients of these reports are likely to discredit them entirely

5. Assume that an analyst is gathering certain types of information which can be obtained only through interrogation of the clientele by means of a questionnaire.
Which one of the following statements that relate to construction of the questionnaire is the MOST valid?

   A. Stress, whenever possible, the use of leading questions.
   B. Avoid questions which touch on personal prejudice or pride.
   C. Opinions, as much as facts, should be sought.
   D. There is no psychological advantage for starting with a question of high interest value.

Questions 6-10.

DIRECTIONS: Questions 6 through 10 consist of sentences lettered A, B, C, and D. For each question, choose the sentence which is stylistically and grammatically MOST appropriate for a management report.

6. A. For too long, the citizen has been forced to rely for his productivity information on the whims, impressions and uninformed opinion of public spokesmen.
   B. For too long, the citizen has been forced to base his information about productivity on the whims, impressions and uninformed opinion of public spokesmen.
   C. The citizen has been forced to base his information about productivity on the whims, impressions and uninformed opinion of public spokesmen for too long.
   D. The citizen has been forced for too long to rely for his productivity information on the whims, impressions and uninformed opinion of public spokesmen.

7. A. More competition means lower costs to the city, thereby helping to compensate for inflation.
   B. More competition, helping to compensate for inflation, means lower costs to the city.
   C. Inflation may be compensated for by more competition, which will reduce the city's costs.
   D. The costs to the city will be lessened by more competition, helping to compensate for inflation.

8. A. Some objectives depend on equal efforts from others, particularly private interests and the federal government; for example, technical advancement.
   B. Some objectives, such as technical advancement, depend on equal efforts from others, particularly private interests and the federal government.
   C. Some objectives depend on equal efforts from others, particularly private interests and the federal government, such as technical advancement.
   D. Some objectives depend on equal efforts from others (technical advancement, for example); particularly private interests and the federal government.

9. A. It has always been the practice of this office to effectuate recruitment of prospective employees from other departments.
    B. This office has always made a practice of recruiting prospective employees from other departments.
    C. Recruitment of prospective employees from other departments has always been a practice which has been implemented by this office.
    D. Implementation of the policy of recruitment of prospective employees from other departments has always been a practice of this office.

10. A. These employees are assigned to the level of work evidenced by their efforts and skills during the training period.
    B. The level of work to which these employees is assigned is decided upon on the basis of the efforts and skills evidenced by them during the period in which they were trained.
    C. Assignment of these employees is made on the basis of the level of work their efforts and skills during the training period has evidenced.
    D. These employees are assigned to a level of work their efforts and skills during the training period have evidenced.

11. To overcome the manual collation problem, forms are frequently padded. Of the following statements which relate to this type of packaging, select the one that is MOST accurate.

    A. Typewritten forms which are prepared as padded forms are more efficient than all other packaging.
    B. Padded forms are best suited for handwritten forms.
    C. It is difficult for a printer to pad form copies of different colors.
    D. Registration problems increase when cut-sheet forms are padded.

12. Most forms are cut from a standard mill sheet of paper.
    This is the size on which forms dealers base their prices. Since an agency is paying for a full-size sheet of paper, it is the responsibility of the analyst to design forms so that as many as possible may be cut from the sheet without waste.
    Of the following sizes, select the one that will cut from a standard mill sheet with the GREATEST waste and should, therefore, be avoided if possible.

    A. 4" x 6"   B. 5" x 8"   C. 9" x 12"   D. 8 1/2" x 14"

13. Assume that you are assigned the task of reducing the time and costs involved in completing a form that is frequently used in your agency. After analyzing the matter, you decide to reduce the writing requirements of the form through the use of ballot boxes and preprinted data.
    If exact copy-to-copy registration of this form is necessary, it is MOST advisable to

    A. vary the sizes of the ballot boxes
    B. stagger the ballot boxes
    C. place the ballot boxes as close together as possible
    D. have the ballot boxes follow the captions

14. To overcome problems that are involved in the use of cut-sheet and padded forms, specialty forms have been developed. Normally, these forms are commercially manufactured rather than produced in-plant. Before designing a form as a specialty form, however, you should be assured that certain factors are present.
Which one of the following factors deserves LEAST consideration?

    A. The form is to be used in quantities of 5,000 or more annually.
    B. The forms will be prepared on equipment using either a pinfeed device or pressure rollers for continuous feed-through.
    C. Two or more copies of the form set must be held together for further processing subsequent to the initial distribution of the form set.
    D. Copies of the form will be identical and no items of data will be selectively eliminated from one or more copies of the form.

15. Although a well-planned form should require little explanation as to its completion, there are many occasions when the analyst will find it necessary to include instructions on the form to assure that the person completing it does so correctly.
With respect to such instructions, it is usually considered to be LEAST appropriate to place them

    A. in footnotes at the bottom of the form
    B. following the spaces to be completed
    C. directly under the form's title
    D. on the front of the form

16. One of the basic data-arrangement methods used in forms design is the *on-line* method. When this method is used, captions appear on the same line as the space provided for entry of the variable data.
This arrangement is NOT recommended because it

    A. forces the typist to make use of document tabs, thus increasing processing time
    B. wastes horizontal space since the caption appears on the writing line
    C. tends to make the variable data become more dominant than the captions
    D. increases the form's processing time by requiring the typist to continually alter margins and indents

17. Before designing a form for his agency, the analyst should be aware of certain basic design standards.
Which one of the following statements relating to horizontal and vertical spacing requirements is *generally* considered to be the MOST acceptable in forms design?

    A. If the form will be completed by computer, no more than four writing lines to the vertical inch should be allowed.
    B. If the form will be completed by hand, allowance should not be made for the different sizes of individual handwriting.
    C. If the form will be completed partly by hand and partly by computer, the analyst should provide the same vertical spacing as for typewriter completion
    D. The form should be designed with proportional spacing for pica and elite type.

18. As an analyst, you may be required to conduct a functional analysis of your agency's forms.
    Which one of the following statements pertaining to this type of analysis is *generally* considered to be MOST valid?

    A. Except for extremely low-volume forms, all forms should be functionally analyzed.
    B. To obtain maximum benefit from the analysis, functional re-analyses of all forms should be undertaken at least once every three to six months.
    C. All existing forms should be functionally analyzed before reorder.
    D. Only new forms should be functionally analyzed prior to being authorized for adoption.

19. The analyst must assure the users of a form that its construction provides for the most efficient method in terms of how data will be entered and processed subsequent to their initial entry.
    While the simplest construction is the cut sheet, the GREATEST disadvantage of this type of construction is

    A. the non-productive *makeready time* required if multiple copies of a form must be simultaneously prepared
    B. the difficulty experienced by users in filling in the forms solely by mechanical means
    C. its uneconomical cost of production
    D. the restrictions of limitations placed on the utilization of a variety of substances which may be used in form composition

20. Assume you have designed a form which requires data to be entered on multiple copies simultaneously. A determination has not yet been made whether to order the form as interleaved-carbon form sets or as carbonless forms.
    The advantage of using carbonless forms is that they

    A. permit more readable copies to be made at a single writing
    B. average about 30 percent lower in price than conventional interleaved-carbon form sets
    C. provide greater security if the information entered on the form is classified
    D. are not subject to accidental imaging

KEY (CORRECT ANSWERS)

1. C
2. B
3. B
4. D
5. B
6. B
7. A
8. B
9. B
10. A
11. B
12. C
13. B
14. D
15. A
16. B
17. C
18. C
19. A
20. C

TEST 2

DIRECTIONS: Each question or incomplete statement is followed by several suggested answers or completions. Select the one that BEST answers the question or completes the statement. *PRINT THE LETTER OF THE CORRECT ANSWER IN THE SPACE AT THE RIGHT.*

1. Many analysts lean toward the use of varying colors of paper in a multiple-part form set to indicate distribution. This usage is GENERALLY considered to be

    A. *desirable;* it is more effective than using white paper for all copies and imprinting the distribution in the margin of the copy
    B. *undesirable;* colored inks should be used instead to indicate distribution in a multipart form set
    C. *desirable;* it will lead to lower costs of form production
    D. *undesirable;* it causes operational difficulties if the form is to be microfilmed or optically scanned

2. After a form has been reviewed and approved by the analyst, it should be given an identifying number. The following items pertain to the form number.
   Which item is MOST appropriately included as a portion of the form number?

    A. Revision date
    B. Order quantity
    C. Retention period
    D. Organization unit responsible for the form

Questions 3-8.

DIRECTIONS: Questions 3 through 8 should be answered on the basis of the following information.

Assume that the figure at the top of the next page is a systems flowchart specifically prepared for the purchasing department of a large municipal agency. Some of the symbols in the flowchart are incorrectly used. The symbols are numbered.

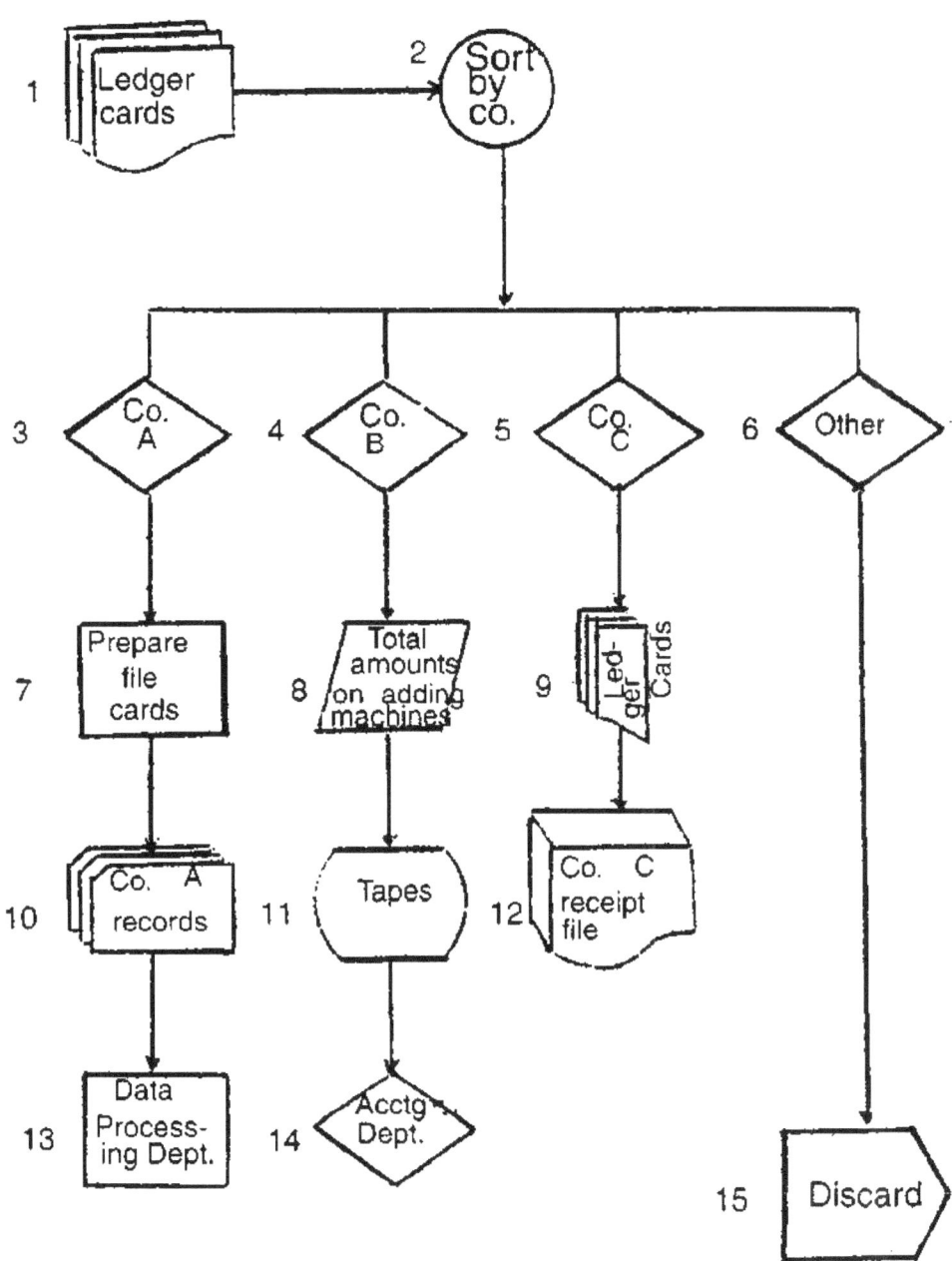

3. According to the flowchart, Number 2 is

   A. *correct*
   B. *incorrect;* the symbol should have six sides
   C. *incorrect;* the symbol should be the same as Number 7
   D. *incorrect;* the symbol should be the same as Number 8

4. According to the flowchart, Number 9 is

   A. *correct*
   B. *incorrect;* the symbol should be the same as Number 1

C. *incorrect;* the symbol should be the same as Number 7
D. *incorrect;* the symbol should be the same as Number 10

5. According to the flowchart, Number 11 is

   A. *Correct*
   B. *incorrect;* the symbol should be the same as Number 13
   C. *incorrect;* the symbol should be the same as Number 10
   D. *incorrect;* the symbol should be the same as Number 9

6. According to the flowchart, Number 14 is

   A. *correct*
   B. *incorrect;* the symbol should have three sides
   C. *incorrect;* the symbol should have six sides
   D. *incorrect;* the symbol should have eight sides

7. According to the flowchart, Number 12 is

   A. *Correct*
   B. *incorrect;* a *file* should be represented in the same form as the symbol which immediately precedes it
   C. *incorrect;* the symbol should be the same as Number 13
   D. *incorrect;* the symbol should be the same as Number 14

8. According to the flowchart, Number 15 is

   A. *correct*

   B. *incorrect;* the symbol should be

   C. *incorrect;* the symbol should be

   D. *incorrect;* the symbol should be

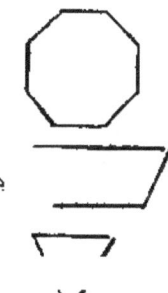

9. An agency expects to increase its services, the workload of the office will increase, and additional equipment and personnel will probably be required. Although there is no set formula for determining how much space will be required in an agency in a specific number of years from now, certain guidelines have been developed to assist the analyst in dealing with the problem of providing expansion space.
   Which of the following statements pertaining to this aspect of space utilization is *generally* considered to be the LEAST desirable practice?

   A. Spread the departments to fit into space that is temporarily surplus and awaiting the day when it is needed
   B. Place major departments where they can expand into the area of minor departments
   C. Visualize the direction in which the expansion will go and avoid placing the relatively fixed installations in the way
   D. Lay out the departments economically and screen off the surplus areas, using them for storage or other temporary usage

Questions 10-11.

DIRECTIONS: Questions 10 and 11 are based on the following layout.

Layout of Conference Room
BUREAU OF RODENT CONTROL

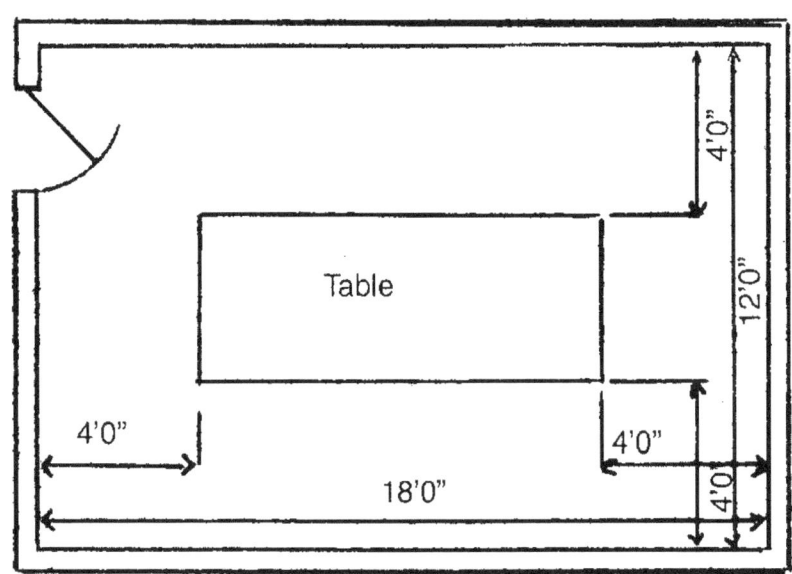

10. The LARGEST number of persons that can be accommodated in the area shown in the layout is
    A. 16 B. 10 C. 8 D. 6

11. Assume that the Bureau's programs undergo expansion and the Director indicates that the feasibility of increasing the size of the conference room should be explored.
    For every two additional persons that are to be accommodated, the analyst should recommend that _____ be added to table length and _____ be added to room length.

    A. 2'-6"; 2'-6"   B. 5'-0"; 5'-0"
    C. 2'-6"; 5'-0"   D. 5'-0"; 2'-6"

Questions 12-14.

DIRECTIONS: Questions 12 through 14 are based on the following information.

SYMBOLS USED IN LAYOUT WORK

Figure I ○
Figure II ─○
Figure III ⊙
Figure IV ⊡
Figure V ─○─
Figure VI ◁
Figure VII (symbol)

Figure VIII (symbol)
Figure IX ─────────
Figure X ─▨──▨──▨─
Figure XI ─▭──▭──▭─
Figure XII ⊠

12. Figure XI is the symbol for
    A. a temporary partition B. floor outlets
    C. ceiling outlets D. a switch

13. A *solid post* is represented by Figure
    A. II B. V C. VIII D. XII

14. Figure VI is the symbol for a(n)
    A. switch B. intercom
    C. telephone outlet D. railing

15. While there is no one office layout that will fit all organizations, there are some reasonably good principles of office layout by function that could be applied to any office situation. Which one of the following statements relating to functions and locations is MOST characteristic of a good layout?
    The
    A. personnel department is usually close to the reception area
    B. purchasing department should be far from the entrance
    C. data processing activity and duplicating services are normally placed together
    D. top management group is usually dispersed throughout the general office group

16. Records are valuable to an organization because recorded information is more accurate and enduring than oral information.
    Of the following, the MOST important stage in records management is at the
    A. storage stage
    B. time when quality control principles are applied
    C. point of distribution
    D. source when records are created

17. The rough layout of an office can be made by sketching the office floor plan from actual measurements, or it can be copied from blueprints furnished by the building management. As an analyst assigned to improve an office layout, you should be aware that the experienced layout man prefers to make his sketch from

    A. a blueprint because it eliminates the extra work in checking a sketch made from it
    B. actual measurements because a blueprint is in a scale of 1/4 or 1/2 inch to a foot instead of the preferred 1/8-inch scale
    C. a blueprint because he can always trust the blueprint
    D. actual measurements because he has to sketch in the desks and other equipment

18. Planning the traffic flow and appropriate aisle space in an office are factors an analyst must consider in any desk arrangement.
    Of the following, it is *generally the* MOST desirable practice to

    A. deny requests to rearrange desks to give employees more working space if the space left for the aisle is more than needed for the traffic
    B. figure operating space and the open file drawer separately from the allowance for the aisle if files must open into the aisle
    C. conserve space by making the main aisle in an office no wider than 36 inches
    D. disregard the length of feeders to an aisle in determining the width of the aisle

19. Code systems which are used to mark records for long- or short-term retention are easy to devise and use.
    Accordingly, of the following situations, it would be MOST appropriate to use the *destroy code* for

    A. information that calls for action within 90 days and for which no record is necessary thereafter
    B. information that may be needed for evaluation of past agency activities
    C. records which contain information that is readily available elsewhere
    D. records that contain information necessary for audit requirements

20. Assume your agency is moving into new quarters and you will assist your superior in assigning space to the various offices. The offices will be air-conditioned. The interior of the space to be assigned is located away from windows.
    Of the following, it is MOST appropriate for you to recommend that the interior of the space be set aside for

    A. legal offices and confidential investigation sections
    B. visitors to the agency
    C. conference and training rooms
    D. typing and stenographic pools

KEY (CORRECT ANSWERS)

1. D
2. A
3. A
4. B
5. D

6. C
7. A
8. C
9. A
10. B

11. A
12. A
13. D
14. C
15. A

16. D
17. D
18. B
19. C
20. C

EXAMINATION SECTION

TEST 1

DIRECTIONS: Each question or incomplete statement is followed by several suggested answers or completions. Select the one that BEST answers the question or completes the statement. *PRINT THE LETTER OF THE CORRECT ANSWER IN THE SPACE AT THE RIGHT.*

1. Several employees complain informally to their supervisor regarding some new procedures which have been instituted.
   The supervisor should IMMEDIATELY
   A. explain that management is responsible
   B. investigate the complaint
   C. refer the matter to the methods analyst
   D. tell the employees to submit their complaint as a formal grievance

   1.____

2. The PRINCIPAL aim of an administrator is to
   A. act as liaison between employee and management
   B. get the work done
   C. keep up morale
   D. train his subordinates

   2.____

3. Work measurement can be applied to operations where workload can be related to
   A. available personnel for the implementation of assigned tasks
   B. follow-up programs for continued progress
   C. cost abatement and optimum efficiency
   D. man hour utilization on assigned tasks

   3.____

4. The one of the following which is NOT a primary advantage of a work measurement program is
   A. the selection of informed personnel
   B. knowledge of personnel needs
   C. support of personnel requests
   D. setting of approximate unit costs

   4.____

5. A program of work measurement would be LEAST likely to
   A. point up the need for management research
   B. keep workload and personnel on an even keel
   C. measure the performance in exceptional operations
   D. evaluate the status of operations

   5.____

6. Generally speaking, there are two kinds of work measurement: (1) the traditional industrial engineering kind where performance standard are determined by time study or other engineering techniques, and (2) the statistical kind where yardsticks (so-called to distinguish them from engineered standard) are developed from a statistical analysis of past performance data. These data consist essentially of periodic reports in which work performed, expressed in identifiable work units, is related to the time required to perform it, usually expressed in man-hours.
The ESSENTIAL difference between the two kinds of work measurement is that
   A. the statistical type if based on past, current, and future determinants of a divergent nature, while engineered standards are restrictive
   B. yardsticks are less restrictive than engineered standards
   C. time study standards employ a higher ratio of man-hour data than do statistical standards
   D. engineered standards are more costly as well as more accurate than routine time study methods

6.____

7. Government has favored the use of the statistical type of work measurement over the industrial type MAINLY because
   A. government is an institution rarely hampered by money-seeking techniques
   B. as the statistical type of work measurement is broadly based, it is more capable of filling the wide expanse of government's needs
   C. employees might object vehemently against speed-ups, thereby sapping work measurement's force
   D. the former appears to be just as effective and less expensive than the latter

7.____

8. A work measurement program is a system by which a
   A. periodic account is kept of individual and group performance
   B. recurring account is kept of group performance
   C. periodic account is kept of performance by an individual
   D. periodic account is kept of performance by a group

8.____

9. Statistical standards developed during the early stages of a work measurement program are
   A. changed too rapidly and thus are of little value in the final program
   B. subject to change as the program moves forward
   C. incorporated into the final program, ultimately for research studies
   D. abandoned before the effective date of the final program

9.____

10. It is NOT an objective of a work measurement program to
    A. furnish a basis for procedural control
    B. provide a true basis for management control
    C. furnish a genuine basis for budget control
    D. provide a basis for management planning

10.____

11. The MOST valid of the following concepts of management control is that it examines
    A. the method with which work assignments have been accomplished in accordance with preconceived plans and policies
    B. preconceived plans and policies to determine their ultimate value
    C. results to determine how well work assignments have been accomplished in accordance with preconceived plans and policies
    D. the work of individual employees to get an acceptable, so as not to endanger the entire control program

12. Of the following, the LEAST likely area in which a deficiency in operations would be revealed by a work measurement program is
    A. improper personnel utilization   B. inadequate equipment
    C. distribution of work   D. personnel rating

13. The MOST accurate of the following statements regarding the standard as used in a work measurement program is:
    A. Standard rates of performance should not be established until the effectiveness of an operation has been determined.
    B. The measure of effectiveness should be kept separate and distinct from the application of standards to actual performance
    C. standards should not be used as guides in planning
    D. Standard rates of performance must be established before effectiveness of an operation can be determined.

14. The first and most important basic consideration in instituting a program of work measurement is the
    A. indoctrination of personnel
    B. establishment of a uniform technology
    C. selection of the time unit
    D. selection of a standard

15. A _____ is an item or a group of items, generally physical, which, when taken in the aggregate, serve to measure amounts of work.
    A. Therblig   B. function   C. operation   D. work unit

16. Which of the following epitomizes the *raison d'etre* of work simplification?
    A. Waste elimination   B. Empirical costs
    C. Time study speed-ups   D. Charting techniques

17. A process charting analysis is likely to be of little value in the event of
    A. a major change in the department's activity
    B. a new supervisor from the outside coming in to head the unit
    C. increase in volume of work
    D. sizable personnel turnover

18. Staff or functional supervision in an organization
    A. is least justified at the operational level
    B. is contrary to the principle of Unity of Command
    C. is more effective than authoritative supervision
    D. normally does not give the right to take direct disciplinary action

19. The correlation between a flow process chart and a flow diagram is BEST described by which of the following statements?
    A. A flow process chart is supportive machinery to the flow diagram.
    B. In essence, the flow process chart exhibits time, distance, and location using standard symbols, whereas the flow diagram exhibits flow lines and uses classification symbols.
    C. Much of the information on the flow process chart is reproduced from the flow diagram.
    D. The flow diagram is complementary to the flow process chart.

20. Indicate which of the following statements is LEAST apt to clarify the underlying distinction between work simplification and other method of betterment procedures.
    Work simplification
    A. is dependent on supervisory participation
    B. is designed for employee participation
    C. emphasizes group participation
    D. emphasizes the ideas of experts

21. In describing the process of administrative management, the LEAST valid description is that it
    A. is composed of interdependent functions
    B. is comprised of related parts
    C. is cyclical
    D. consists of independent parts

22. Work activity, as to type, individual performance, and time expenditure, is BEST illustrated by a _____ chart.
    A. flow process   B. work flow
    C. work distribution   D. operations

23. Neither the work distribution nor the flow process chart furnishes adequate intelligence as to
    A. methods   B. activities
    C. nature of work activity D. unit prices

24. A graphic presentation of the steps and distribution through which each copy of a multiple copy office form travels is a(n)
    A. work distribution chart B. flow process chart
    C. flow diagram   D. operations chart

25. A CHIEF target of work simplification is 25._____
    A. the achievement of greater productivity with the same effort
    B. obtaining the same work accomplishment with less effort
    C. employee participation and little resistance to change
    D. all of the above

KEY (CORRECT ANSWERS)

1.	B		11.	C
2.	B		12.	D
3.	D		13.	D
4.	A		14.	B
5.	C		15.	D
6.	B		16.	A
7.	D		17.	B
8.	B		18.	D
9.	B		19.	D
10.	A		20.	D

21.	D
22.	C
23.	D
24.	C
25.	C

TEST 2

DIRECTIONS: Each question or incomplete statement is followed by several suggested answers or completions. Select the one that BEST answers the question or completes the statement. *PRINT THE LETTER OF THE CORRECT ANSWER IN THE SPACE AT THE RIGHT.*

1. In conducting a work simplification program, which of the following office problems is the MOST likely to be solved by the use of the flow process chart?
    A. Are the employee deluged with unrelated tasks?
    B. What activities are the most costly, in terms of time consumed?
    C. Is the proper sequence of work activity employed?
    D. Is there an even distribution of work among the employees?

    1.____

2. In the matter of procedural analysis, which question should be asked FIRST?
    A. When should the step be performed?
    B. Who should perform the step?
    C. What is the significance of the step?
    D. Where can this be improved upon?

    2.____

3. Storage on a movement diagram is represented by
    A. ◇   B. ▽   C. ▢   D. all of the above

    3.____

4. The use of a flow process chart is LESS desirable in indicating
    A. the time rate for each step   B. distance traveled
    C. equipment-facilities layout   D. sequence of activities

    4.____

5. Division of work is BEST delineated by means of a _____ chart.
    A. work methods   B. flow process
    C. work distribution   D. flow authority

    5.____

6. In seeking to conduct a work simplification analysis, the MOST appropriate first step would be to
    A. chart the procedures
    B. survey the facilities as to spatial access
    C. make problem area determination
    D. set up composition of forms analysis

    6.____

7. The conception of a standard is BEST denoted as a
    A. hypothetical level   B. circumscribed level of work activity
    C. level of comparing   D. quintessential idea

    7.____

8. With reference to office work simplification, it could be considered expedient to
    A. first simplify the procedure and then the individual methods
    B. simplify the individual methods first, then the procedure
    C. concurrently, simplify the methods and the procedure
    D. none of the above

    8.____

9. The MOST valid precept relative to work analysis is
   A. the volume of work is inversely proportional to the distribution or sequence of work
   B. in meeting production standards, the sequence of work transcends its distribution
   C. work sequence and work distribution should be analyzed in relation to work volume
   D. work sequence and work distribution should be examined for work validation concepts

10. The flow process chart is PRINCIPALLY used
    A. as a useful tool to train new employees
    B. to ascertain the effectiveness of the organization's employees
    C. to pinpoint *bottlenecks* affecting an operation
    D. to determine the visibility of organizational relationships

11. The work distribution chart would generally be of little value in answering which of the following questions?
    A. In what order are the activities being carried out?
    B. Which activities consume the most time?
    C. Is a work balance maintained among the employees?
    D. Are the employees laboring under a plethora of unrelated tasks?

12. A worthwhile analytical tool in work simplification is the flow process chart. The MOST valid description is that
    A. a flow process chart is generally reliable without review for a period of a year
    B. the flow process chart should be reviewed and possibly revised at six-month intervals
    C. the flow process chart is an ad hoc instrument
    D. the value of a flow process chart is not determined by time

13. In the analysis of a method of procedure in a work simplification program, a competent analyst should FIRST focalize on the clearance or diminution of
    A. verifications   B. transportations
    C. inspections   D. storages

14. Which one of the following statements BEST distinguishes a method from a procedure?
    A. A method is a consistent sequence of procedures.
    B. A procedure comprises a sequence of related methods, performed in most instances by a single person.
    C. A series of related methods comprise a procedure.
    D. In breadth, a method takes precedence over a procedure.

15. The data provided by the flow process chart in a work simplification program is INADEQUATE to answer which one of the following questions?
    A. What is being performed?
    B. In what manner should the work be performed?
    C. What is the quantity of work performed?
    D. Who should perform the work?

Questions 16-17.

DIRECTIONS: Questions 16 and 17 are to be answered on the basis of the following passage.

Ideally, then, the process of budget formulation would consist of a flow of directives down the organization, and a reverse flow of recommendations in terms of alternatives among which selection would be made at every level. Ideally, also, a change in the recommendations at any level would require reconsideration and revision at all lower levels. By a process of successive approximation, everything would be taken into account and all points of view harmonized. Such a process, however, would be ideal only if the future could be foreseen clearly and time did not matter. As it is, in a complicated organization like the Federal government, the initial policy objectives established for the budget become out-of-date, before such a procedure could be carried through. While this difficulty does not in any way impugn the principle that the budget should be considered in terms of alternatives, it may call for short-cut methods of estimation rather than long drawn-out ones.

16. According to the above passage,
    A. the ideal method for estimating purposes is a short one
    B. the ideal method is not ideal for use in the Federal government
    C. directive should flow up and down via short methods
    D. the Federal government needs to speed up its reverse flow of recommendations for greater budgetary estimates

17. A suitable title for the above passage would be:
    A. Formulating the Federal Government's Budgetary Principles
    B. Directives and Recommendations: Budgetary Flow
    C. The Process of Budget Formulation
    D. The Application of the Ideal Estimate to the Federal Government

Questions 18-19.

DIRECTIONS: Questions 18 and 19 are to be answered on the basis of the following passage.

For purpose of budget formulation, the association of budgeting with accounting is less fortunate. Preparing for the future and recording the past do not necessarily require the same aptitudes or attitudes. The task of the accountant is to record past transactions in meticulous detail. Budgeting involves estimates of an uncertain future. But, because of the influence of accounts, government's budgets are prepared in a degree of detail that is quite unwarranted by the uncertain assumptions on which the estimates are based. A major source of government waste could be eliminated if estimates were prepared in no greater detail than was justified by their accuracy.

18. The author of the above paragraph
    A. is undermining the accounting profession
    B. believes accountants dwell solely in the past and cannot deal with the future efficiently
    C. wants the accountants out of government unless they become more accurate in their findings
    D. wishes to redirect the accountants' handling of budget procedures

18.____

19. The author's attitude appears to be
    A. tongue-in-cheek   B morose
    C. strident   D. constructive

19.____

20. The idea that classic organizational structure tends to create work situations having requirements counter to those for psychological success and self-esteem, sometimes called the *organizational dilemma*, is MOST closely associated with
    A. Argyris   B. Taylor   C. Gulick   D. Maslow

20.____

Questions 21-25.

DIRECTIONS: Questions 21 through 25 contain incorrectly used words which change the meaning of the statement. Identify the word in the statement that is incorrect and select the choice that would make the sentence correct.

21. Standards of production performance are necessary to reveal the quantities of material, the number of hours of labor, the machine hours, and quantities of service (as, for example, power, steam, etc.) necessary to perform the various production operations. The establishment of such standards is an engineering rather than an accounting task, but it should be emphasized that such standards are needless to the development of the budgetary procedure—at least insofar as the budget is to serve as a tool of control. Such standards serve not only in the development of the budget and in measuring efficiency of production performance, but also in developing purchase requirements and in estimating costs.
    A. Manifest   B. Evaluation   C. Essential   D. Function

21.____

22. Where standard costs are not available or their use is impracticable due to uncertainty of prices, estimates of the costs must be made on the basis of past experience and expected conditions. Ability to use standards largely eliminates the use of the budget for purposes of control of costs but its value remains for purposes of coordination of the program with purchases and finance.
    A. Failure   B. Current   C. Culmination   D. Apparent

22.____

23. While one of the first objectives of the labor budget is to provide the highest practicable degree of regularity of employment, consideration must also be given to the estimating and perdurability of labor cost. Regularity of employment in itself effects some reduction in labor cost, but when carried beyond the point of practicality, it may increase other costs. For example, additional sales effort may be required to expand sales volume or to develop new products for slack periods; the cost of carrying inventories and the dangers of obsolescence and price declines must also be considered. A proper balance must be secured.
    A. Material   B. Control   C. Futures   D. To

23._____

24. The essentials of budgeting perhaps can be summarized in this manner:
    I. Develop a sound business program
    II. Report on the progress in achieving that program
    III. Take necessary action as to all variances which are inevitable
    IV. Revise the program to meet the changing conditions as required

    A. Perfect   B. Plans   C. Controllable   D. Secure

24._____

25. If a planning and control procedure is considered worthwhile, then it is a syllogism that preparation for the installation should be adequate. Time devoted to this educational aspect ordinarily will prove quite rewarding. The management to be involved with the budget, and particularly the middle management, must have a clear understanding of the budgetary procedure.
    A. Acquired   B. Remedial   C. Monetary   D. Truism

25._____

KEY (CORRECT ANSWERS)

1.	D		11.	A
2.	C		12.	D
3.	D		13.	D
4.	C		14.	C
5.	C		15.	C
6.	C		16.	B
7.	C		17.	C
8.	A		18.	D
9.	C		19.	D
10.	C		20.	A

21. C
22. B
23. B
24. C
25. D

TEST 3

DIRECTIONS: Each question or incomplete statement is followed by several suggested answers or completions. Select the one that BEST answers the question or completes the statement. *PRINT THE LETTER OF THE CORRECT ANSWER IN THE SPACE AT THE RIGHT.*

1. The MOST important element in job satisfaction is
   A. job security
   B. responsibility or recognition
   C. salary
   D. type of supervision

   1.____

2. The point of view that the average person wishes to avoid responsibility, wishes to be directed, as little ambition, and wants security above all, is described by Douglas MacGregor as Theory
   A. X
   B. Y
   C. Z
   D. X and Y combined

   2.____

3. To prepare a work distribution chart, two other types of lists must generally be prepared.
   In usual order of preparation, they are a(n) _____ and a(n) _____ list.
   A. flow chart; activity
   B. skills list; task
   C. task list; activity
   D. activity list; task

   3.____

4. A statistical control program in an office is valuable to direct deterioration in operations.
   It is, however, LEAST likely to reveal
   A. when preventative action is needed
   B. when a variation is due to chance
   C. when an assignable cause is present
   D. what the cause of error or deterioration is

   4.____

5. Which of the following BEST defines an organization chart?
   An organizational chart
   A. depicts informal channels of communication within an organization
   B. depicts the major functions of an organization and the normal work flow between subdivisions of the organization
   C. presents graphically the arrangement and interrelationships of the subdivisions and the functions of the organization as they exist
   D. presents graphically the arrangement and relationships of all the positions authorized in an organization

   5.____

6. In considering an office layout for a unit, which of the following factors should generally receive the LEAST consideration?
   A. Lighting levels in the existing area
   B. Major work flow—the processing of paper
   C. Present and projected growth rate of the unit
   D. Traffic patterns of employees and visitors

   6.____

7. The BEST way to secure effective management is usually to 7.____
   A. allow staff to help solve administrative problems of line management
   B. provide a good organization structure
   C. select capable managers
   D. set up conservative spans of control

8. Which of the following is NOT an advantage of oral instruction as compared 8.____
   with written instructions?
   Oral
   A. instructions can be easily changed
   B. instructions are superior in transmitting complex directives
   C. instructions facilitate exchange of information between a supervisor and his subordinate(s)
   D. discussions are possible with oral instructions, making it easier to ascertain understanding

9. Which organization principle is MOST closely related to procedural analysis 9.____
   and improvement?
   A. Duplication, overlapping, and conflict should be eliminated.
   B. The objectives of the organization should be clearly defined.
   C. Managerial authority should be clearly defined.
   D. Top management should be freed of burdensome details.

10. Of the following control techniques, a _____ is MOST useful on large, complex 10.____
    projects.
    A. general work plan   B. Gantt chart
    C. monthly progress report   D. PERT chart

11. Work is organized so that the work is broken down into a series of jobs. 11.____
    Each unit of work moves progressively from position to position until completion.
    This paragraph BEST describes a
    A. parallel plan of work subdivision   B. serial plan
    C. unit assembly plan   D. unit process plan

12. According to the classic studies of Rensis Likert, the GREATEST factor making 12.____
    for good morale and increased productivity was having a
    A. good program of employee benefits and wage scales
    B. supervisor who gave his employees free rein after they were fully trained and did not interfere with them
    C. supervisor who was primarily interested in production
    D. supervisor who, while interested in production, was primarily *employee-centered*

13. The managerial grid shows two concerns and a range of interaction between them.
In this grid, the horizontal axis indicates a concern for _____ and the vertical axis indicates a concern for _____.
    A. production; people
    B. hierarchy; people
    C. organization; people
    D. people; costs

14. It has been decided to make a few important revisions in the methods and procedures of a particular work unit.
Of the following, which method of implementing these revisions would probably be the MOST desirable in terms of morale and of efficiency?
    A. Give all employees in unit individual instructions in the revised procedures and make sure each employee knows them before instructing the next
    B. Institute all revisions at once, followed by on-the-job training for all members of the work unit
    C. Introduce the revisions one at a time and accompany each revision with an orientation for employees
    D. Set up a training course for the employees which instructs them in all aspects of the revised procedures prior to their implementation

15. An operations research technique which would be employed to determine the optimum number of window clerks or interviewers to have in an agency serving the public would MOST likely be the use of
    A. line of balance
    B. queueing theory
    C. simulation
    D. work sampling

16. Douglas MacGregor's theory of human motivation classifies worker behavior into two distinct categories: Theory X and Theory Y. Theory X, the traditional view, states that the average man dislikes working and will avoid work if he can, unless coerced. Theory Y holds essentially the opposite view.
The manager can apply both of these theories to worker behavior BEST if he
    A. follows an *open-door* policy only with respect to his immediate subordinates
    B. recognizes his subordinates' mental and social needs as well as agency needs
    C. recognizes that executive responsibility is primarily limited to fulfillment of agency productivity goals
    D. directs his subordinate managers to follow a policy of close supervision

17. In interpersonal communications, it is important to ascertain whether oral directions and instruction are understood.
One of the MOST important sources of such information is known as
    A. the *halo* effect
    B. evaluation
    C. feedback
    D. quantitative analysis

18. The *grapevine* MOST often provides a useful service by
    A. correcting some of the deficiencies of the formal communication system
    B. rapidly conveying a true picture of events
    C. involving staff in current organizational changes
    D. interfering with the operation of the formal communication system

19. People who are in favor of a leadership style in which the subordinates help make decisions contend that it produces favorable effects in a work unit. According to these people, which of the following is NOT likely to be an effect of such *participative management*?
    A. Reduced turnover
    B. Accelerated learning of duties
    C. Greater acceptance of change
    D. Reduced appearance of the work unit's goals

20. Employees of a public service agency will be MOST likely to develop meaningful goals for both the agency and the employee and become committed to attaining them if supervisors
    A. allow them unilaterally to set their own goals
    B. provide them with a clear understanding of the premises underlying the agency's goals
    C. encourage them to concentrate on setting only short-range goals for themselves
    D. periodically review the agency's goals in order to suggest changes in accordance with current conditions

KEY (CORRECT ANSWERS)

1.	B	11.	B
2.	A	12.	D
3.	C	13.	A
4.	D	14.	D
5.	C	15.	B
6.	A	16.	B
7.	B	17.	C
8.	B	18.	A
9.	A	19.	D
10.	D	20.	B

EXAMINATION SECTION
TEST 1

DIRECTIONS: Each question or incomplete statement is followed by several suggested answers or completions. Select the one that BEST answers the question or completes the statement. *PRINT THE LETTER OF THE CORRECT ANSWER IN THE SPACE AT THE RIGHT.*

1. In organizational theory, the optimum span of control, that is, the number of subordinates who can be effectively supervised by one man above the level of the first line supervisor is GENERALLY set at between
    A. 3 and 6   B. 6 and 12   C. 12 and 18   D. 18 and 24

    1.____

2. Which of the following is LEAST desirable as a basic guide to normal conventional office layout?
    A. Arrange desks so that work flows in a normal fashion
    B. Place files nearest to the persons who will use them
    C. Utilize a number of small areas to provide privacy
    D. Utilize one single large area

    2.____

3. *A set of objects together with relationships between the objects and between their attributes* is the definition of
    A. a perceptual whole and its subcomponents
    B. a system in the terms of specific systems theory
    C. an organism
    D. forms control

    3.____

4. A technique of time study in which each employee maintains a record of his own time is GENERALLY known as _____ study.
    A. estimated time   B. observed time
    C. time log   D. wristwatch

    4.____

5. An employee has approached a supervisor with a request for a change involving his personal status or with a suggestion for making an improvement in the work The supervisor knows that the suggestion cannot be granted.
    Of the following, the BEST procedure would be for the supervisor to
    A. refer the matter to the personnel department
    B. refer the matter to his superior for action
    C. reject the proposal, explaining the defects or objections which cannot be overcome
    D. shelve the idea so that the employee will realize it cannot be acted upon

    5.____

6. There are, in general, a number of common methods of drawing samples for statistical work.
    The method in which a regularly ordered interval is maintained between the items chosen is BEST termed _____ sampling.
    A. random   B. stratified or selective
    C. systematic   D. work

    6.____

7. The multi-column process chart can be put to all of the following general uses EXCEPT to
   A. improve office layout
   B. improve procedures
   C. standardize procedures
   D. train personnel

8. If one wished to show the percentage of change over a period of time, the MOST appropriate type of graph or chart GENERALLY would be the _____ chart.
   A. bar
   B. line or curve
   C. logarithmic or semilogarithmic
   D. pie

9. A chart designed for the explicit purpose of portraying graphically information relating to the degree of responsibility of key individuals for the performance of various functions is BEST described as a(n) _____ chart.
   A. linear responsibility
   B. work distribution
   C. work process
   D. staff

10. The technique of work measurement LEAST useful for setting up a program of office incentive pay GENERALLY would be
    A. log sheets
    B. stopwatch time study
    C. wristwatch time study
    D. work sampling

11. There are a number of steps to be taken in making a work sampling study in order to set production standards. Three of the steps listed below are peculiar only to work sampling, in contrast with other work measurement techniques.
    The one EXCEPTION is:
    A. Define the breakdown of work into the proper elements of work and no-work or delay to be observed
    B. Determine the required number of observations needed for the specified degree of reliability
    C. Establish the observation intervals
    D. Make a preliminary estimate of work and no-work or delay element percentages for step A

12. A number of standardized flow process chart symbols have been generally accepted.
    The symbol $\bar{v}$ GENERALLY indicates a(n)
    A. delay
    B. storage or file
    C. inspection
    D. operation

13. The number of standardized flow process chart symbols have been generally accepted.
    The symbol ▭ GENERALLY indicates a(n)
    A. delay
    B. storage or file
    C. inspection
    D. operation

14. The type of work for which short interval scheduling generally would be LEAST applicable would be the work of a group of
    A. calculating clerks
    B. order clerks
    C. technically-oriented clerks
    D. typists

15. In writing a business report, the BEST expression to use, in general, of those listed below would NORMALLY be:
    A. Because
    B. Inasmuch as
    C. In view of the fact that
    D. With reference to

16. Of the following, the MAJOR advantage of a random access data processing system, as compared with a sequential-type system, is its
    A. ability to use more than one input system
    B. demand for more sophisticated systems and programming
    C. greater storage capacity and access speed
    D. potential for processing data on a *first come, first-served* basis

17. A good rule to remember with regard to decision making is that decisions should be made
    A. at the highest level competent to make such a decision
    B. at the lowest level competent to make such a decision
    C. by the person responsible for carrying out the decision
    D. by the person responsible for the work of the unit

18. Which of the following potential systems would LEAST likely be improved by being online? A(n) _____ system.
    A. budgeting control
    B. welfare eligibility
    C. employee payroll
    D. inventory control

19. A management information and control system essentially should be designed to provide management personnel with up-to-date information which will enable them to improve control over their operations.
    In designing such a system, the FIRST step to determine is:
    A. What information is needed to effectively control operations?
    B. What information is presently available?
    C. What organization changes are necessary to implement the system?
    D. Who is presently processing the information that might be used?

20. In designing control reports, which of the following guidelines is of MOST importance?
    A. Financial information should always be carried to the nearest penny.
    B. The report should be a simple and concise statement of only the pertinent facts.
    C. The report should indicate the source of original data and how the computations were made.
    D. The report should have the broadest possible distribution at all levels of management.

21. A situation which enables a number of users at offsite locations to have access to an office computer network is called
    A. multiprocessing
    B. multiprogramming
    C. cloud connectivity
    D. remote access

    21._____

22. Computer software that would typically be used for widespread dissemination of a business report is
    A. Microsoft Word
    B. Microsoft PowerPoint
    C. Adobe Elements
    D. Google Sheets

    22._____

23. Which of the following steps is LEAST desirable in designing an electronic data processing system?
    A. Design the EDP system first, then relate it to current operations
    B. Develop a corollary chart for the corresponding flow of information
    C. Develop a flow chart for the functions affected by the system
    D. Obtain from available EDP equipment that which best fits current operations

    23._____

24. Electronic data processing equipment can produce more information faster than can be generated by any other means. Because this is true, one wonders whether our ability to generate information has not far outstripped our ability to assimilate it.
    In view of this, a PERSISTENT danger management faces is in
    A. determining the budget for management information systems
    B. determining what information is of real worth
    C. finding enough computer personnel
    D. keeping their computers fully occupied

    24._____

25. The one of the following that is an ADVANTAGE of a hybrid local/remote network setup over fully local access is
    A. the ability to access a network outside normal circumstances
    B. closer oversight of personnel
    C. more efficient workflow
    D. reduced costs for software and production equipment

    25._____

KEY (CORRECT ANSWERS)

1. A
2. C
3. A
4. C
5. C

6. C
7. A
8. C
9. A
10. A

11. A
12. B
13. C
14. C
15. A

16. D
17. B
18. C
19. A
20. B

21. D
22. A
23. A
24. B
25. A

TEST 2

DIRECTIONS: Each question or incomplete statement is followed by several suggested answers or completions. Select the one that BEST answers the question or completes the statement. *PRINT THE LETTER OF THE CORRECT ANSWER IN THE SPACE AT THE RIGHT.*

1. In analyzing data for the acquisition of new equipment, an analyst gathers the facts, analyzes them, and develops new procedures which will be required when the new equipment arrives.
Inn analyzing the factors involved, which one of the following is normally LEAST important in the evaluation of new equipment?
   A. Cost factors
   B. Layout and installation factors
   C. Production planning
   D. Operational experience of manufacturers of allied equipment

1.____

2. If an analyst is required to recommend the selection of a machine for an office operation, he can BEST judge the expected output of a particular machine by pursuing which of the following courses of action?
Obtain
   A. an actual test run of the machine in his office
   B. data from the manufacturer of the machine
   C. information on the percentage of working time the machine will be used
   D. the experience of actual users of similar machines elsewhere

2.____

3. Of the following, the BEST definition of records management is
   A. storage of all types of records at minimum expense
   B. planned control of all types of records
   C. storage of records for maximum accessibility
   D. systematic filing of all types of records

3.____

4. The one of the following which is NOT a primary objective of a records retention and disposal system is to
   A. assure appropriate preservation of records having permanent value
   B. dispose of records not warranting further preservation
   C. establish retention standards for archives
   D. provide an opportunity to use miniaturization

4.____

5. Of the following functions of management, the one which should NORMALLY precede the others is
   A. coordinating   B. directing   C. organizing   D. planning

5.____

6. One of the more famous studies of organizations is called the Hawthorne study.
This work was one of the first to point out the importance of
   A. employee's benefit and retirement programs
   B. informal organization among employees
   C. job engineering
   D. styles of position classification

6.____

7. In organization theory, the type of position in which an individual is appointed to give technical aid to management on a particular problem area is generally BEST termed a(n)
   A. administrative assistant
   B. assistant to
   C. staff assistant
   D. staff specialist

8. In organizing, doing what works in the particular situation, with due regard to both short- and long-range objective, is BEST termed
   A. ambivalence
   B. authoritarianism
   C. decentralization
   D. pragmatism

9. If an effort were made to reduce the number of private offices in a new layout, the LEAST effective substitute in offering privacy would be the use of
   A. an open area with lower movable partitions or railings separating each individual
   B. conference rooms
   C. larger desks
   D. modular desk units

10. The term *administrative substation* NORMALLY refers to
    A. a work station handling a number of office services for an office organization
    B. a work station where middle level supervisors are located
    C. an office for handling management trainees
    D. the functions allocated to particular levels of administrative managers

11. An operations research technique which would be applied to determine the optimum number of window clerks or interviewers to have in an agency serving the public would MOST likely be the use of
    A. line of balance
    B. queuing theory
    C. simulation
    D. work sampling

12. A type of file which permits the operator to remain seated while the file can be moved backward and forward as required is BEST termed a _____ file.
    A. lateral
    B. movable
    C. reciprocating
    D. rotary

13. The technique of work measurement in which the analyst observes the work at random times of the day is BEST termed
    A. indirect observation
    B. logging
    C. ratio delay
    D. wristwatch

14. Examples of predetermined time systems generally should include all of the following EXCEPT
    A. Master Clerical Data
    B. Methods Time Measurement
    C. Short Interval Data
    D. Work Factor

15. A technique by which the supervisor or an assistant distributes a predetermined batch of work to the employee at periodic intervals of the day is generally BEST known as
    A. backlog control scheduling
    B. production control scheduling
    C. short interval schedule
    D. workload balancing

16. E. Wright Bakke defined his *fusion process* as: The
    A. work environment to some degree remakes the organization and the organization to some degree remakes the work environment
    B. fusing of the interests of both management and labor unions
    C. community of interest between first line supervisors and top management
    D. organization to some degree remakes the individual and the individual to some degree remakes the organization

17. A pamphlet on issues related to 2020s-era office setup would likely be titled
    A. Close Encounters: How Proximity Elevates Production
    B. How Connectivity Spurs Inspiration
    C. See Your Employees in a New Light With Open Floor Plans
    D. From A to Zoom: The Terminology of the Hybrid Workplace

18. In planning office space for a newly established bureau, it would usually be LEAST desirable to
    A. concentrate, rather than disperse, the chief sources of office noises
    B. design an office environment with the same brightness as the office desk
    C. designate as reception rooms, washrooms, and other service areas those areas that will receive lesser amounts of illumination than those areas in which private office work will be performed
    D. eliminate natural light in cases where it is not the major light source

19. A private office should be used when its use is dictated by facts and unbiased judgment. It should never be provided simply because requests and sometimes pressure have been brought to bear.
    Of the following reasons used to justify use of a private office, the one that requires the MOST care in determining whether a private office is actually warranted is
    A. an office has always been provided for a particular job
    B. prestige considerations
    C. the confidential nature of the work
    D. the work involves high concentration

20. Theoretically, an ideal organization structure can be set up for each enterprise. In actual practice, the ideal organization structure is seldom, if ever, obtained.
    Of the following, the one that normally is of LEAST influence in determining the organization structure is the
    A. existence of agreements and favors among members of the organization
    B. funds available
    C. opinions and beliefs of top executives
    D. tendency of management to discard established forms in favor of new forms

21. An IMPORTANT aspect to keep in mind during the decision-making process is that
    A. all possible alternatives for attaining goals should be sought out and considered
    B. considering various alternatives only leads to confusion
    C. once a decision has been made, it cannot be retracted
    D. there is only one correct method to reach any goal

    21._____

22. Implementation of accountability requires
    A. a leader who will not hesitate to take punitive action
    B. an established system of communication from the bottom to the top
    C. explicit directives from leaders
    D. too much expense to justify it

    22._____

23. Of the following, the MAJOR difference between systems and procedures analysis and work simplification is:
    A. The former complicates organizational routine and the latter simplifies it
    B. The former is objective and the latter is subjective
    C. The former generally utilizes expert advice and the latter is a *do-it-yourself* improvement by supervisors and workers
    D. There is no difference other than in name

    23._____

24. Systems development is concerned with providing
    A. a specific set of work procedures
    B. an overall framework to describe general relationships
    C. definitions of particular organizational functions
    D. organizational symbolism

    24._____

25. Organizational systems and procedures should be
    A. developed as problems arise as no design can anticipate adequately the requirements of an organization
    B. developed jointly by experts in systems and procedures and the people who are responsible for implementing them
    C. developed solely by experts in systems and procedures
    D. eliminated whenever possible to save unnecessary expense

    25._____

KEY (CORRECT ANSWERS)

1.	D		11.	B
2.	A		12.	C
3.	B		13.	C
4.	D		14.	C
5.	D		15.	C
6.	B		16.	D
7.	D		17.	D
8.	D		18.	D
9.	C		19.	A
10.	A		20.	D

21. A
22. B
23. C
24. B
25. B

TEST 3

DIRECTIONS: Each question or incomplete statement is followed by several suggested answers or completions. Select the one that BEST answers the question or completes the statement. *PRINT THE LETTER OF THE CORRECT ANSWER IN THE SPACE AT THE RIGHT.*

1. The CHIEF danger of a decentralized control system is that
   A. excessive reports and communications will be generated
   B. problem areas may not be detected readily
   C. the expense will become routine
   D. this will result in too many *chiefs*

   1.____

2. Of the following, management guides and controls clerical work PRINCIPALLY through
   A. close supervision and constant checking of personnel
   B. spot checking of clerical procedures
   C. strong sanctions for clerical supervisors
   D. the use of printed forms

   2.____

3. Which of the following is MOST important before conducting fact-finding interviews?
   A. Becoming acquainted with all personnel to be interviewed
   B. Explaining the techniques you plan to use
   C. Explaining to the operating officials the purpose and scope of the study
   D. Orientation of the physical layout

   3.____

4. Of the following, the one that is NOT essential in carrying out a comprehensive work improvement program is
   A. standards of performance   B. supervisory training
   C. work count/task list   D. work distribution chart

   4.____

5. Which of the following control techniques is MOST useful on large complex systems projects?
   A. A general work plan   B. Gantt chart
   C. Monthly progress report   D. PERT chart

   5.____

6. The action which is MOST effective in gaining acceptance of a study by the agency which is being studied is
   A. a directive from the agency head to install a study based on recommendations included in a report
   B. a lecture-type presentation following approval of the procedures
   C. a written procedure in narrative form covering the proposed system with visual presentations and discussions
   D. procedural charts showing the *before* situation, forms, steps, etc. to the employees affected

   6.____

7. Which of the following is NOT an advantage in the use of oral instructions as compared with written instructions? Oral instruction(s)
   A. can easily be changed
   B. is superior in transmitting complex directives
   C. facilitate exchange of information between a superior and his subordinate
   D. with discussions make it easier to ascertain understanding

8. Which organization principle is MOST closely related to procedural analysis and improvement?
   A. Duplication, overlapping, and conflict should be eliminated.
   B. Managerial authority should be clearly defined.
   C. The objectives of the organization should be clearly defined.
   D. Top management should be freed of burdensome detail.

9. Which one of the following is the MAJOR objective of operational audits?
   A. Detecting fraud
   B. Determining organization problems
   C. Determining the number of personnel needed
   D. Recommending opportunities for improving operating and management practices

10. Of the following, the formalization of organization structure is BEST achieved by
    A. a narrative description of the plan of organization
    B. functional charts
    C. job descriptions together with organization charts
    D. multi-flow charts

11. Budget planning is MOST useful when it achieves
    A. cost control
    B. forecast of receipts
    C. performance review
    D. personnel reduction

12. The UNDERLYING principle of sound administration is to
    A. base administration on investigation facts
    B. have plenty of resources available
    C. hire a strong administrator
    D. establish a broad policy

13. Although questionnaires are not the best survey tool the management analyst has to use, there are times when a good questionnaire can expedite the *fact-finding* phase of a management survey.
    Which of the following should be AVOIDED in the design and distribution of the questionnaire?
    A. Questions should be framed so that answers can be classified and tabulated for analysis.
    B. Those receiving the questionnaire must be knowledgeable enough to accurately provide the information desired.

C. The questionnaire should enable the respondent to answer in a narrative manner.
D. The questionnaire should require a minimum amount of writing.

14. Of the following, the formula which is used to calculate the arithmetic mean from data grouped in a frequency distribution is M =

    A. $\dfrac{N}{\Sigma fx}$ B. $N(\Sigma fx)$ C. $\dfrac{\Sigma fx}{N}$ D. $\dfrac{\Sigma x}{fN}$

15. Arranging large groups of numbers in frequency distributions
    A. gives a more composite picture of the total group than a random listing
    B. is misleading in most cases
    C. is unnecessary in most instances
    D. presents the data in a form whereby further manipulation of the group is eliminated

16. After a budget has been developed, it serves to
    A. assist the accounting department in posting expenditures
    B. measure the effectiveness of department managers
    C. provide a yardstick against which actual costs are measured
    D. provide the operating department with total expenditure to date

17. Of the following, which formula is used to determine staffing requirements?

    A. $\dfrac{\text{Hours per man-day}}{\text{Volume x Standard}}$ = Employees Needed

    B. $\dfrac{\text{Hours per man-day x Standard}}{\text{Volume}}$ = Employees Needed

    C. $\dfrac{\text{Hours per man-day x Volume}}{\text{Standard}}$ = Employees Needed

    D. $\dfrac{\text{Volume x Standard}}{\text{Hours per man-day}}$ = Employees Needed

18. Of the following, which formula is used to determine the number of days required to process work?

    A. $\dfrac{\text{Employees x Daily Output}}{\text{Volume}}$ = Days to Process Work

    B. $\dfrac{\text{Employees x Volume}}{\text{Daily Output}}$ = Days to Process Work

    C. $\dfrac{\text{Volume}}{\text{Employees x Daily Output}}$ = Days to Process Work

    D. $\dfrac{\text{Volume x Daily Output}}{\text{Employees}}$ = Days to Process Work

19. Identify this symbol, as used in a Systems Flow Chart.
    A. Document
    B. Decision
    C. Preparation
    D. Process

20. Of the following, the MAIN advantage of a form letter over a dictated letter is that a form letter
    A. is more expressive
    B. is neater
    C. may be mailed in a window envelope
    D. requires less secretarial time

21. The term that may be defined as a *systematic analysis of all factors affecting work being done or all factors that will affect work to be done, in order to save effort, time, or money* is
    A. flow process charting
    B. work flow analysis
    C. work measurement
    D. work simplification

22. Generally, the LEAST important basic factor to be considered in developing office layout improvements is to locate
    A. office equipment, reference facilities, and files as close as practicable to those using them
    B. persons as close as practicable to the persons from whom they receive their work
    C. persons as close as practicable to windows and/or adequate ventilation
    D. persons who are friendly with each other close together to improve morale

23. Of the following, the one which is LEAST effective in reducing administrative costs is
    A. applying objective measurement techniques to determine the time required to perform a given task
    B. establishing budgets on the basis of historical performance data
    C. motivating supervisors and managers in the importance of cost reduction
    D. selecting the best method—manual, mechanical, or electronic—to process the essential work

24. *Fire-fighting* is a common expression in management terminology.
    Of the following, which BEST describes *fire-fighting* as an analyst's approach to solving paperwork problems?
    A. A complete review of all phases of the department's processing functions
    B. A studied determination of the proper equipment to process the work
    C. An analysis of each form that is being processed and the logical reasons for its processing
    D. The solution of problems as they arise, usually at the request of operating personnel

25. Assume that an analyst with a proven record of accomplishment on many projects is having difficulties on his present assignment.
Of the following, the BEST course of action for his superior to take is to
   A. assume there is a personality conflict involved and transfer the analyst to another project
   B. give the analyst some time off
   C. review the nature of the project to determine whether or not the analyst is equipped to handle the assignment
   D. suggest that the analyst seek counseling

25.____

KEY (CORRECT ANSWERS)

1. B
2. D
3. C
4. B
5. D

6. C
7. B
8. A
9. D
10. C

11. A
12. A
13. C
14. C
15. A

16. C
17. D
18. C
19. A
20. D

21. D
22. D
23. B
24. D
25. C

EXAMINATION SECTION
TEST 1

DIRECTIONS: Each question or incomplete statement is followed by several suggested answers or completions. Select the one that BEST answers the question or completes the statement. *PRINT THE LETTER OF THE CORRECT ANSWER IN THE SPACE AT THE RIGHT.*

1. If an analyst recommends to the head of a newly established agency that the latter institute a line type of organization, he should also point out that this structure has the following MAJOR disadvantage:
    A. Delay will be encountered in reaching decisions.
    B. Coordination will be difficult to secure.
    C. Authority and responsibility will be diffused.
    D. Discipline will be hard to maintain.

1.____

2. Of the following statements which relate to the use of office space, the one that is LEAST valid is:
    A. A request for a conference room on the basis of privacy for meetings usually cannot be justified, for most private offices are suitable for meetings.
    B. Private offices are objectionable because they tend to slow up the work by interfering with supervisory effectiveness.
    C. The reception room should not handle ordinary and necessary traffic between different areas in the office.
    D. The space utilization of private offices is about 35 to 50 percent of that of the open area arrangement.

2.____

3. In preparing the layout for a small office, PARAMOUNT consideration should be given to a design that will
    A. accommodate the flows representing the largest volumes of work
    B. cause work to progress through its production cycle regardless of backtracking in a straight line or U
    C. increase the speed and movement of papers involved in the flow of work to the shortest compass feasible
    D. take into account vertical relationships of floor locations in the work flow

3.____

4. When centralization of office activities is instituted, which one of the following conditions will MOST likely occur?
    A. Confidentiality of office work will decrease.
    B. Equitable wage schedules will be undermined.
    C. Office machine maintenance costs will increase.
    D. Training of office employees will be delayed.

4.____

5. Descriptor is a term COMMONLY used in
    A. information retrieval   B. network analysis
    C. planning and forecasting   D. systems analysis

5.____

6. Of the following, the BEST way to secure effective management is USUALLY to
   A. allow staff agencies to help solve the administrative problems of line management
   B. provide a good organization structure
   C. select capable managers and administrators
   D. set up conservative spans of control

7. The MOST effective way of graphically representing the division of total costs into component costs as they vary over a period of time is by means of a
   A. band chart   B. pictograph
   C. pie diagram   D. histogram

8. During the past 50 years, the rate of increase in the number of office workers has been much greater than that of our total working force.
   The LEAST likely reason to cause this increase is the
   A. dispersal of clerical operations which accompanied the growth in manufacturing
   B. development of "service industries"
   C. use of more factual information by managers
   D. expansion in business legislation and governmental regulatory agencies

9. In attempting to discover flaws in an organization, an organization chart has been prepared.
   The condition that will be LEAST likely to be disclosed through use of the organization chart will be
   A. executives who are burdened with details
   B. work schedules that are unmet
   C. promotional possibilities that are not being provided
   D. functions which are becoming secondary due to splitting among departmental units

10. The PRIMARY function of systems analysis in the Planning Programming Budgetary System is to
    A. cost out various alternatives
    B. develop a PERT chart for evaluating program content
    C. develop better alternatives than those which are in the currently approved program
    D. provide perspective in judging the validity of an expenditure

11. Systems analysis would be LEAST effective in solving which of these problems? The
    A. determination of need for a new pier
    B. problem of air pollution
    C. selection of a site for a police station
    D. selection of engineering personnel

12. In procedural analysis, when the purpose of a particular step has been shown to be justifiable to the end purpose of the procedure, the NEXT necessary step is usually to
    A. determine the time limits for the step
    B. weigh the value of the step against the expense involved
    C. sell the idea to the supervisory staff
    D. make it a part of the procedure

12.____

13. ▽ is a symbol used in records management flow diagrams to indicate
    A. destruction of paper   B. filing and/or permanent storage
    C. inspection   D. microfilming is necessary

13.____

14. The concept that decisions should be made at the lowest level in an organization where all the (required) information and competence are available is MOST particularly a general rule in
    A. communications theory   B. decentralization of authority
    C. incremental decision-making D. span of control

14.____

15. An office quality control program may comprise several approaches. The one LEAST desirable of the following normally is to
    A. follow a policy of spot or sample checking
    B. follow a practice of 100% checking of all work to verify its correctness
    C. inspect the work by means of a statistical quality control program
    D. review and tally errors being detected from present checking operations to determine the amount of checking presently being followed and the results being obtained

15.____

16. When a form is to be completed by an electronic data processing machine, which of the following is LEAST necessary?
    A. Form number   B. Form title   C. Lines   D. Margins

16.____

17. Under a PPBS system, the selection of the proper alternative program should be made by the
    A. administrator responsible for the program, with the approval of the mayor and city legislative body
    B. budget director, basing his decision according to the optimum alternative
    C. budget examiner who reviews the administration budget
    D. chief systems analyst who programmed the alternatives

17.____

18. Which of the following is LEAST applicable in describing PPBS as a general concept? A
    A. quantitative method of budgeting for the coming year
    B. system of defining long-range alternative programs and planning the allocation of resources on the basis of the cost of the long-range program versus the benefit derived over the planning period
    C. system of measuring budgeted performance against pre-established goals
    D. system that establishes the importance of a program in terms of the expected cost of executing

18.____

19. Under a PPBS system, substantive planning is NORMALLY defined as
    A. fiscal planning
    B. planning of future budgets
    C. planning of objectives—ultimate and intermediate
    D. planning of programs—ultimate and intermediate

20. The method of selection which would provide the TIGHTEST standard under the logging method of work measurement would be
    A. one-third array			B. modal average
    C. selected arithmetic average	D. upper quartile

21. A concept for the evaluation of managers whereby goals are set and agreed upon for each manager, and then his attainment of those goals is evaluated at a particular prearranged target date, is BEST termed
    A. management by objectives
    B. management evaluation planning
    C. managerial performance appraisal
    D. program evaluation

22. When work is organized so that the work is broken into a series of jobs, and each unit of work (a customer order, invoice, etc.) moves progressively to position until completion, we would NORMALLY refer to this as the
    A. parallel plan of work subdivision	B. serial plan
    C. unit assembly plan			D. unit process plan

23. The type of organization in which employees report to a nominal manager for administrative purposes but are assigned to *ad hoc* supervisors as various assignments arise is BEST termed the _____ type of organization.
    A. functional			B. process
    C. project or task force		D. unit assembly

24. The expression which BEST defines a generalized situation in which several programs may be executed simultaneously or concurrently is
    A. multiprocessing			B. multiprogramming
    C. on-line, real time programming	D. process overlap

25. The sampling technique which consists of taking selections at constant intervals (every nth unit) from a list of the universe is called _____ sampling.
    A. area			B. quota
    C. stratified random	D. systematic

26. A method of project scheduling and control which shows the MOST optimistic, MOST pessimistic, and MOST probable estimate of time for how long each task in a project will take is called
    A. CPM (Critical Path Method)	B. Gantt charting
    C. Linear Responsibility Charting	D. PERT

27. The idea that classic organizational structure tends to create work situations having requirements counter to those for psychological success and self-esteem, sometimes called the "organizational dilemma," is MOST closely associated with which one of the following persons?
    A. Chris Argyris
    B. Frederick Taylor
    C. Luther Gulick
    D. Max Weber

28. Charles J. Hitch is known PRIMARILY for his work in the area of
    A. administrative behavior
    B. behavioral sciences
    C. organizational analysis
    D. PPBS

Questions 29-30.

DIRECTIONS: Questions 29 and 30 are to be answered on the basis of the following paragraph.

If one were to observe the information, in all its variant forms, that flows to a manager in the typical American enterprise, he would have a word for it: chaos. Subordinates want to be helpful, or to promote themselves, or to reflect discredit somewhere, and they originate or serve as a transmission belt for information they think the manager should have. Furthermore, it is the nature of the business process that information is generated where it is most easily reflected and is very scarce in areas or phases where data are not readily available. If one could project a tape which showed information density through time, he would find areas of heavy concentration and areas of little or no cloudiness. This means two things: First, people seem to have an inner drive to report available information in many ways, many forms, and for many users. Note what an accountant or statistician can do with two figures—or a mathematician without any figures at all! Second, the lack of information in specific areas means only that it is not available; it does not mean that it is unnecessary. Indeed, the blind areas may be of the greatest importance for decision-making purposes.

29. The result of the state of affairs described in the above paragraph would MOST likely be
    A. inconsequential
    B. an impetus to proper decision-making
    C. high costs and poor decisions
    D. a successful uniform information system

30. The author in this paragraph is PRIMARILY concerned with
    A. decision-making theory
    B. communications
    C. tape information systems
    D. information gathering by accountants and statisticians

KEY (CORRECT ANSWERS)

1.	B	11.	D	21.	A
2.	A	12.	B	22.	B
3.	A	13.	B	23.	C
4.	A	14.	B	24.	B
5.	A	15.	B	25.	D
6.	C	16.	C	26.	D
7.	A	17.	A	27.	A
8.	A	18.	A	28.	D
9.	B	19.	C	29.	C
10.	C	20.	D	30.	B

TEST 2

DIRECTIONS: Each question or incomplete statement is followed by several suggested answers or completions. Select the one that BEST answers the question or completes the statement. *PRINT THE LETTER OF THE CORRECT ANSWER IN THE SPACE AT THE RIGHT.*

1. It has been decided to make a few important revisions in the methods and procedures of a particular work unit.
   Of the following, the method of implementing these revisions which would probably be MOST desirable in terms of morale as well as efficiency is to
   A. give all the employees in the work unit individual instructions in the revised procedures, making sure that each employee fully understands the changes before instructing the next employee
   B. institute all the revisions at once, followed by on-the-job training for all the employees in the work unit
   C. introduce the revisions one at a time, accompanying each revision with an orientation for the employees
   D. set up a training course for the employees, instructing them in all aspects of the revised procedures prior to their implementation

   1.____

2. In an administrative survey of a multiple-unit organization, which of the following is it usually MOST important to identify? The
   A. data and information used commonly by units, how used and by whom
   B. flow of data and information within a single organization unit
   C. type and volume of data used within individual units and transmitted between units
   D. way data and information are transmitted between units, how used and by whom

   2.____

3. A noted authority has described a common method of making organizational policy in which the decision-maker tries to find some acceptable level of goal accomplishment short of ultimate fulfillment of all objectives and to frame policies toward such fulfillment.
   Of the following, this method is BEST termed
   A. feedback   B. incrementalism
   C. satisfying   D. seriality

   3.____

4. The managerial grid, as defined by Blake and Mouton, shows two concerns and a range of interaction between them as follows: The horizontal axis indicates a concern for _____, while the vertical axis indicates a concern for _____.
   A. hierarchy; people   B. production; people
   C. organization; people   D. people; P/L (profit or loss)

   4.____

53

5. In the managerial grid, which managerial style is dominant for any given person in any particular situation can be determined by any one or several sets of conditions in combination.
   The five conditions in CORRECT order are:
   A. Organization, management, values, chance, production
   B. Organization, situation, values, personality, chance
   C. Production, situation, personality, chance, individually
   D. Values, personality, variety, organization, chance

6. The analyst may be faced with a choice of either recommending service contracts or recommending on-call service for maintenance of equipment.
   In making a decision, the one of the following factors which would mitigate MOST against the use of on-call service would be that
   A. equipment utilization is not heavy
   B. prompt service when breakdowns occur is seldom essential
   C. regular checkups and servicing are considered desirable based on past equipment history
   D. trade-ins are made frequently

7. The type of paper stock MOST commonly used for office forms work is _____ bond.
   A. cotton content B. duplicating or mimeo
   C. rag   C. sulphite

8. In laying out an office, according to most authorities, the amount of space which NORMALLY should be allowed for a clerk would in the range of _____ square feet.
   A. 10 to 15   B. 25 to 100   C. 110 to 125   D. 130 to 150

9. A noted behavioral scientist believes that the MOST important element in job satisfaction, of those listed below, s
   A. job security   B. responsibility or recognition
   C. salary   D. type of supervision

10. The point of view that the average human being prefers to be directed, wishes to avoid responsibility, has relatively little ambition, and wants security above all has been described in Douglas MacGregor's classic book on human motivation in business.
    He includes this point of view in what he calls
    A. Theory X   B. Theory Y
    C. Theory Z   D. Theory X and Y combined

11. New desk top electronic machines are of two main types—printing or display. Display type machines show the results by any of the following methods EXCEPT for
    A. cathode ray tube   B. electro-mechanical
    C. mosaic or liquid crystal D. nixie

12. The type of chart that is normally MOST useful for studying the work assignments and job content of individual positions in a particular organizational unit when making a procedure analysis is the _____ chart.
    A. columnar flow
    B. procedure flow
    C. work distribution
    D. work process

13. To prepare a work distribution chart, two other types of lists generally must be prepared.
    In the usual order of preparation, they are FIRST a(n)
    A. flow diagram, then an activity list
    B. skills list, then a task list
    C. task list, then an activity list
    D. activity list, then a task list

14. The critical path is defined as that path (or those paths) through a network
    A. showing the least number of time units
    B. showing the greatest number of time units
    C. which consists (or consist) entirely of sequential activities
    D. which links (or link) together activities in concurrent relationship to each other

15. A statistical quality control program in the office is valuable in alerting management that the level of quality for particular transactions has deteriorated.
    It is, however, LEAST likely to reveal
    A. when preventive action is necessary
    B. when a variation is due to other than chance
    C. when an assignable cause is present
    D. what the cause of the error is

16. In work measurement, the value of a TMU is _____ min.
    A. .0001   B. .0006   C. .0036   D. .0100

17. The sheet version of microfilm is NORMALLY referred to as
    A. microfiche   B. micro-sheet   C. microdupe   D. microspec

18. While a line and staff organization is generally considered to have the advantages of both a line organization and a functional organization, with the disadvantages of each eliminated, disadvantages, nevertheless, do exist.
    Of the following, the one that describes the MOST significant disadvantage of a line and staff type of organization is that
    A. fewer opportunities are afforded to match the capacities of personnel with the job, since a smaller number of jobs is required
    B. line orders and staff advice, although clearly known to managers, tend to be confused by non-management members
    C. staff officers may attempt to take over line authority
    D. staff officers may tend to follow the ideas of the line officers and not generate their own ideas

19. Which activities take the most time? Are skills being utilized properly? Are employees doing too many unrelated tasks?
Of the following, the BEST technique to find answers to all of these questions is the
    A. flow diagram
    B. skills chart
    C. work count
    D. work distribution chart

20. Operator participation in management improvement work is LEAST likely to do which one of the following?
    A. Assure the use of the best available management techniques
    B. Make installation of new procedures quicker and easier
    C. Overcome the stigma of the outside expert
    D. Take advantage of the desire of most operators to seek self-improvement

21. Which of the following BEST defines an organization chart? A
    A. chart depicting the informal channels of communications within an organization
    B. chart depicting the major functions of an organization and the normal work flow between subdivisions of the organization
    C. graphic presentation of the arrangement and interrelationships of the subdivisions and functions of an organization as they exist
    D. graphic presentation of the arrangement and relationships of al positions authorized in an organization

22. Under a PPBS system, fiscal planning is NORMALLY considered to be planning
    A. for anticipated fixed costs only
    B. for present personnel requirements, procurement, and construction
    C. of current income and expenditures
    D. of future budgets

23. In the selection of space within an office building, LEAST consideration, generally, should be given to which of the following factors?
    A. Future expansion
    B. Proximity to elevators and restrooms
    C. Stability of other tenants on other floors
    D. Ventilation

24. In office layout, an office unit consisting of a combined desk and file cabinet and small movable partitions may BEST be described as _____ unit.
    A. conference
    B. landscaped office
    C. modular office
    D. semi-private office

25. Which of the following is it generally MOST important to consider when allocating office space?
    A. Actual organizational relationships
    B. Lighting requirements
    C. Noise levels
    D. Preferences of employees with over ten years of seniority

26. In preparing office layouts, the one of the following general factors within the affected unit which should generally receive the LEAST consideration is
    A. lighting levels in the existing area
    B. major work flow—the processing of paper
    C. present and projected growth rate of the unit
    D. traffic patterns of employees and visitors

27. In reviewing a new office layout, the one of the following questions that should normally receive LEAST consideration is:
    A. Have several alternate move day plans been prepared showing possible new locations of each piece of office equipment?
    B. Has expansion been provided for?
    C. Have alternate schemes been adequately explored to try to achieve the best possible layout?
    D. Is there adequate aisle space for ingress and egress?

28. Which of the following is the LEAST important reason for preparing a written study report? The
    A. report documents findings and recommendations so that the client can review and comment on them
    B. report is of interest as an historical document
    C. report serves as a document useful in implementing the recommendations
    D. writing process itself helps the analyst structure his thinking and conclusions

29. According to the classic studies by Rensis Likert at the University of Michigan, the GREATEST factor making for good morale and increased productivity was having a
    A. good program of employee benefits and wage scales
    B. supervisor who gave his employees free rein, after they were fully trained, and did not interfere with them
    C. supervisor who was interested primarily in production
    D. supervisor who, while also interested in production, was primarily "employee-centered"

30. Organization structure deals with the relationship of functions and the personnel performing these functions. It is usually advisable to think first of functions, then of the individuals performing these functions.
    MOST implicit in this approach is the recognition that
    A. conditions outside the organization may necessitate changes in the organization structure
    B. functions need not always be coordinated for an organization to effectively carry out its objectives
    C. functions tend to change with time while the interests and abilities of personnel are usually permanent
    D. personnel emphasis often results in unusual combinations of duties that are difficult to manage

KEY (CORRECT ANSWERS)

1.	D	11.	B	21.	C
2.	A	12.	C	22.	D
3.	C	13.	C	23.	C
4.	B	14.	A	24.	C
5.	B	15.	D	25.	A
6.	C	16.	B	26.	A
7.	D	17.	A	27.	A
8.	B	18.	C	28.	B
9.	B	19.	D	29.	D
10.	A	20.	A	30.	D

EXAMINATION SECTION

TEST 1

DIRECTIONS: Each question or incomplete statement is followed by several suggested answers or completions. Select the one that BEST answers the question or completes the statement. *PRINT THE LETTER OF THE CORRECT ANSWER IN THE SPACE AT THE RIGHT.*

1. The new head of a central filing unit, after studying a procedure in use, decided that it was unsatisfactory. He thereupon drew up an entirely new procedure which made no use of and ignored the existing procedure.
   This plan of action is, in general,
   A. *satisfactory*; a new broom sweeps clean
   B. *unsatisfactory*; any plan should use available resources to the utmost before resorting to new creation
   C. *satisfactory*; in general, use of part of an old procedure and part of a new procedure results sin an unworkable patchwork arrangement
   D. *unsatisfactory*; before deciding that the existing procedure was unusable, he should have requested that an independent, unbiased agency study the problem
   E. *satisfactory*; it is usually less time consuming to construct a new plan than to remedy an old one

   1.____

2. Assume that you have broken a complex job into simpler and smaller components.
   After you have assigned a component to each employee, should you proceed to teach each employee a number of alternative methods for doing his job?
   A. *yes*; the more methods for performing a job an employee knows, the more chance there is that he will choose the one best suited to his abilities
   B. *No*; experienced employees should be permitted to decide how to perform the jobs assigned to them
   C. *Yes*; if several different methods are available, a desirable flexibility of operation results
   D. *No*; a single method for each job should be decided upon and taught
   E. *Yes*; the employees will have greater interest in their jobs

   2.____

3. Assume that you are the head of a major staff unit and that a line unit has requested from your unit a special report to be completed in one day. After reviewing the request, you decide that much tie would be saved if two items which you know are superfluous are omitted from the report. You discuss the matter with the head of the other unit and he still insists that the two items are essential for his purposes.
   The one of the following actions which you should take at this stage is to
   A. plan to complete the report, including the two items, as expeditiously as possible
   B. write a memorandum to the department head giving both opinions fairly and asking for a decision

   3.____

C. plan to complete the report without the two items, as expeditiously as possible
D. devise a plan for preparing the report without the two items which will permit you to add them later if they prove necessary although some time may be lost
E. again review the report with the line unit showing them why the two items are unnecessary

4. The one of the following functions of a supervisor which can be MOST successfully delegated is
   A. responsibility for accomplishing the unit's mission
   B. handling discipline
   C. checking completed work
   D. reporting to the bureau chief
   E. placing subordinates in the proper job

4.____

5. It is a standard operating procedure in an office which receives several thousand forms each week to have the file on clerk accumulate a week's receipts before filing them. The forms will not be examined for a period of one month after receipt.
   In comparison with daily filing, this procedure is, in general,
   A. *less satisfactory*; it keeps the files unnecessarily incomplete
   B. *more satisfactory*; it tends to reduce filing time
   C. *less satisfactory*; all information should be placed in a safe storage place as soon as possible
   D. *more satisfactory*; it tends to eliminate the prefiling period
   E. *less satisfactory*; it tends to build up an unnecessary period

5.____

6. Some organizations attempt to keep a constant backlog of work.
   This procedure is usually
   A. *undesirable*; reports are not ready when they are needed
   B. *desirable*; it tends to insure continuity of work flow
   C. *undesirable*; production records are too difficult to keep
   D. *desirable*; it tends to keep the employees under constant pressure
   E. *undesirable*; it tends to keep the employees under constant pressure

6.____

7. The first few times a procedure is carried through, a close check should be kept of all work times.
   The PRIMARY reason for this is to
   A. be able to present a clear picture of the situation
   B. determine if the employees understand the procedure
   C. evaluate the efficiency which may have been presented by the new procedure
   D. determine the efficiency of the employees
   E. permit revision of schedules

7.____

8. The one of the following pieces of information which is of LEAST importance in setting up the schedule for a given job is the time
   A. which is required to perform each component of the job
   B. when the source material will be available
   C. the job will take under adverse conditions
   D. by which the job must be completed
   E. employees will be available

9. Every employee should have a thorough knowledge of the organization of which he is a part.
   Of the following, the BEST justification for the above opinion is that
   A. the feeling of being a member of a team develops a responsible attitude toward one's everyday duties
   B. in an emergency, an employee may be called upon to perform duties other than his own
   C. the intricate details of an organization as complicated as a city department cannot easily be reduced to an organization chart
   D. an understanding of the different specialized units in an organization is often necessary to achieve the organization's given objective
   E. many city jobs are technical; thus, each employee should be trained to have more than a single narrow skill

10. The one of the following which is NOT a good rule in administering discipline is for you as a supervisor to
    A. reprimand the employee in private even though the fault was committed before others
    B. allow the employee a chance to reply to your criticism if he wishes
    C. be as specific as possible in criticizing the employee for his faults
    D. be sure you have all the facts before you reprimand an employee for an error he has committed
    E. allow an extended period to elapse after an error has been committed before reprimanding an employee

11. After you have submitted your annual evaluations of the work of your subordinates, one of them whose work has not been satisfactory complains to you that your evaluation was unjustified.
    For you to avoid discussing the evaluation but to point out two or three specific instances where the employee's work was below standard is
    A. *desirable*; an employee should be told what aspects of his work are unsatisfactory
    B. *undesirable*; once the evaluation has been submitted, there is no point in reconsidering it
    C. *desirable*; once the evaluation has been submitted, there is no point in reconsidering it but a discussion of the employee's weaknesses may help
    D. *undesirable*; it would have been better to explain how you arrived at your evaluation
    E. *desirable*; entering into a general argument is bad for the discipline of an organization

12. The chief of a central files bureau which has 50 employees customarily spends 12.____
a considerable portion of his time in spot-checking the files, reviewing material
being transferred from active to inactive files and similar activities.
From the viewpoint of the department top management, the MOST pertinent
evaluation which can be made on the basis of this information is that the
    A. supervisor is conscientious and hardworking
    B. bureau may need additional staff
    C. supervisor has not made a sufficient delegation of authority and
       responsibility
    D. bureau needs an in-service training course as the work of its employees
       requires an abnormal amount of review
    E filing system employed may be inadequate

13. Assume that you are in charge of a unit with 40 employees. The department 13.____
head requests immediate preparation of a special and rather complicated
report which will take about a day to complete if everyone in your unit works on
it.
After breaking the job into simple components and assigning each component
to an employee, should more than one person be instructed on the procedure
to be followed on each component?
    A. *No*; the procedure would be a waste of time in this instance
    B. *Yes*; it is always desirable to have a replacement available in the event of
       illness or any other emergency
    C. *No*; in general, as long as an employee's job performance is satisfactory,
       there is no need to train an alternate
    D. *Yes*; the presence of more than one person in a unit who can perform a
       given task tends to prevent the formation of a bottleneck
    E. *No*; there is, in general, no need to train more than one employee in the
       performance of a special job

14. A new employee who has shown that she is capable of performing superior work 14.____
during the first month of her employment falls far below this standard after the
first month.
For the supervisor to wait until the end of the probationary period and then
recommend that she be discharged if her work is still unsatisfactory is
    A. *undesirable*; she should have been discharged when her work became
       unsatisfactory
    B. *desirable*; there is no place in the civil service for unsatisfactory
       employees
    C. *undesirable*; he should immediately attempt to determine the cause of the
       poor performance
    D. *desirable*; the employee is entitled to an opportunity to prove herself
    E. *undesirable*; the employee is obviously capable of performing good work
       and simply requires some guidance from the supervisor

15. In order to make sure that work is completed on time, the unit supervisor should 15.____
    A. use the linear method of delegating responsibility
    B. pitch in and do as much of the work himself as he can
    C. schedule the work and keep himself informed of its progress
    D. not assign more than one person to any one task
    E. know the capabilities of his subordinates

16. One of the more effective ways to obtain optimum performance from employees 16.____
    is to keep them off balance by not letting them feel secure in the job; to permit
    an employee to feel secure is to invite him to settle into a comfortable rut.
    The point of view expressed in this statement is
    A. *correct*; studies have shown that the degree of effort put forth on a job
       generally varies directly with the degree of job insecurity
    B. *incorrect*; studies have shown that a relatively high degree of security is
       conducive to best job performance
    C. *correct*; while studies have shown that there is little relationship between
       security and job performance, what tendencies are present to support the
       point of view expressed
    D. *incorrect*; studies have shown that there is little relationship between
       security and job performance and what tendencies are present are
       opposed to the point of view expressed
    E. *correct*; while no specific studies have been made in this field, analogous
       studies made in similar fields show that permitting a feeling of security to
       develop results in decreased job performance

Questions 17-19.

DIRECTIONS: Questions 17 through 19 are to be answered on the basis of the following
            paragraph.

The supervisor of a large clerical and statistical division has assigned to one of the units
under his supervision the preparation of a special statistical report required by the department
head. The unit accepted the assignment without comment but soon ran into considerable
difficulty because no one in his unit had had any statistical training.

17. If a result of this lack of training is that the report is not completed on time, 17.____
    although everyone has done all that could be expected, the responsibility for
    the failure rests with
    A. the department head   B. the supervisor
    C. the unit head   D. the employees in the unit
    E. no one

18. This incident indicates that the supervisory staff has insufficient knowledge of 18.____
    employee
    A. capabilities
    B. reaction to increased demands
    C. on-the-job training needs
    D. work habits
    E. ability to perform ordinary assignments

19. After working on the report for two days, the unit head notifies the supervisor that he will not be able to get the report out in the required time. He states that his staff will be completely trained in another day or two and that after preparing the report will be a simple matter. At this stage, the supervisor decides to have the statistical unit prepare the report.
    This action on the part of the supervisor is
    A. *undesirable*; the unit head should be given an incentive to continue with his training program which may produce good results
    B. *desirable*; it is the most effective way in which the supervisor can show his displeasure with the unit head's failure
    C. *undesirable*; it may adversely affect the morale of the unit
    D. *desirable*; it will generally result in a better report completed in a shorter time
    E. *undesirable*; the time spent training the unit will be completely wasted

19.____

20. A supervisor criticizes a subordinate's work by telling him that he is disappointed with it. The supervisor states that the work is completely unsatisfactory, shows where it is bad, and says that improvement is expected.
    This approach is usually
    A. *good*; the employee knows just where he stands
    B. *poor*; some favorable comment should be made at the same time if possible
    C. *good*; it is good policy to keep this type of interview as short as possible
    D. *poor*; the employee should be asked to explain why his work is poor
    E. *good*; the supervisor did not criticize the subordinate in front of other employees

20.____

Questions 21-25.

DIRECTIONS: Column I below lists five kinds of statistical data which are to be transformed into a chart or a graph for incorporation into the department annual report. Column II lists nine different kinds of graphs or charts. For each type of information listed in Column I, select the chart or graph from Column II by means of which it should be demonstrated.

COLUMN I   COLUMN II

21. The relationship between employees' occupational classification and their salaries, for all employees by occupational classification, showing minimum, maximum, and average salary in each group.

22. A comparison of the number of employees in the department, the departmental budget the number of employees in the operating divisions and the operating division budget for each year over a ten-year period.

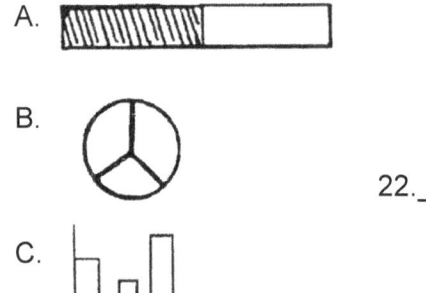

21.____

22.____

COLUMN I	COLUMN II
23. The amount of money spent for each of the department's 10 most important functions during the past year.	D.  23.____
24. The percentage of the department's budget spent for each of the department's activities for each year over a ten-year period.	E. 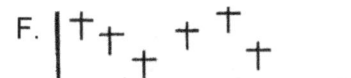 24.____
25. The number of each kind of employee employed in the department over a period of twenty years and the total number of employees in the department for each of these periods.	F.  25.____
	G. 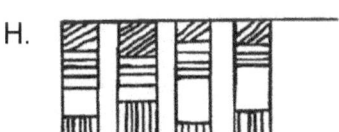
	H. 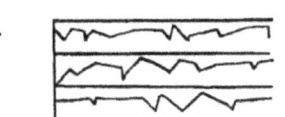
	I.

KEY (CORRECT ANSWERS)

1.	B	11.	D
2.	D	12.	C
3.	A	13.	A
4.	C	14.	C
5.	B	15.	C
6.	B	16.	B
7.	E	17.	B
8.	C	18.	A
9.	A	19.	D
10.	E	20.	B

21. F
22. D
23. C
24. H
25. G

TEST 2

DIRECTIONS: Each question or incomplete statement is followed by several suggested answers or completions. Select the one that BEST answers the question or completes the statement. *PRINT THE LETTER OF THE CORRECT ANSWER IN THE SPACE AT THE RIGHT.*

1. The report of the head of Unit Y to his bureau chief on the performance of a new clerical employee indicates that the performance is not up to the expected standard. After reading the report, the bureau chief transferred the employee to Unit X.
   This action on the part of the bureau chief was
   A. in line with good personal practice; an employee who does poorly in one place may do better in another
   B. premature; an attempt to discover the cause of the poor performance should be made first
   C. desirable; personnel reports become meaningless unless acted upon at once
   D. undesirable; unsatisfactory employees should be dismissed and not transferred from unit to unit
   E. in the best interest of the organization; whenever a supervisor cannot get along with a subordinate for whatever reason, it is desirable to transfer the subordinate

2. Suppose that you have been consulted by a department head who wishes to initiate an in-service training course in his department. The department head suggests that, as a first step, a training course be initiated for supervisors in the department.
   This suggestion is BEST characterized as
   A. *undesirable*; the supervisors are generally the persons least in need of work incentives
   B. *desirable*; it is generally cheaper and more effective to train a few supervisors than a large number of employees
   C. *undesirable*; supervisors may be held up to ridicule if they are isolated for training
   D. *desirable*; trained supervisors are needed to train employees
   E. *undesirable*; employees should be trained before supervisors

3. Any person thoroughly familiar with the specific steps in a particular class of work is well qualified to serve as a training course instructor in that work.
   This statement is erroneous CHIEFLY because
   A. it is practically impossible for any instructor to be acquainted with all the specific steps sin a particular class of work
   B. what is true of one class of work is not necessarily true of other types of work
   C. a qualified instructor cannot be expected to have detailed information about many specific fields

D. the steps in any type of work are usually interrelated and not independent or unique
E. the quantity of information possessed by an instructor does not bear a direct relationship to the quality of instruction

4. Of the following, the MOST significant argument against making it compulsory for civil service employees to attend a training course is that
   A. unwilling trainees will be penalized in any event by non-promotion
   B. most training requires additional time and expense on the part of the trainee
   C. training is highly desirable but not absolutely essential for adequate job performance
   D. incompetent work is generally reflected in poor service ratings
   E. trainees must be receptive if training is to be successful

5. There are four basic systems of job evaluation which have been extensively used by government and industry.
   The one of the following which is NOT one of these is the _____ system.
   A. Benchmark
   B. Factor Comparison
   C. Point
   D. Job Classification
   E. Ranking

6. Of the following, the CHIEF advantage derived by filling all vacancies in an organization by promotion from below rather than from outside the organization is that such a procedure
   A. fills existing vacancies from the widest possible recruitment base
   B. stimulates individual employees to improve their work habits
   C. avoids personality difficulties likely to arise when an employee is assigned to supervise former colleagues
   D. indirectly coordinates the work of different units by interchange of personnel
   E. encourages reorientation and review of administrative procedures

7. Of the following, the CHIEF justification for a periodic classification audit is that
   A. salaries should be readjusted at frequent intervals
   B. some degree of personnel turnover should always be expected
   C. a career service requires regular promotion opportunities
   D. employees require frequent stimulation and encouragement
   E. positions frequently change over a period of time

8. A classification analyst sorts jobs horizontally and vertically.
   Of the following, the LEAST important job factor to be considered with respect to vertical placement is
   A. independence of action and decision
   B. consequence of errors
   C. kind and character of work performed
   D. degree of supervision received
   E. determination of policy

9. Assume that you have been assigned to prepare a plan for conducting a large scale job classification survey.
Of the following, the BEST suggestion for reducing the number of appeals from the final allocations likely to be received after the classification study has been completed is to
   A. have supervisors check statements of employees on classification questionnaires
   B. allocate present positions to proposed classes according to jurisdictional assignments
   C. adjust salary to present level of work performed by employees
   D. allow employee participation throughout the classification process
   E. postpone controversial problems until simpler problems have been solved and a general blueprint laid down

10. A comment made by an employee about a training course was, *Oh, I suppose it's important for the job but it's a waste of time for me just to sit in that course and yawn while the instructor rambles on."*
The fundamental error in training methodology to which this criticism points is failure to provide
   A. goals for the students
   B. for individual differences
   C. connecting links between new and old material
   D. for student participation
   E. motivation for the subject matter of the course

11. You are preparing a long report addressed to your superior on a study which you have conducted for him.
The one of the following sections which should come FIRST in the report is a
   A. description of the working procedure utilized in the study
   B. description of the situation which exists
   C. summary of the conclusions of the survey
   D. discussion of possible objections to the report and their refutation
   E. description of the method of installing the recommendations

12. While setting up a reporting system to help the department planning section, an administrator proposed the policy that no overlap or duplication be permitted even if it meant that some minor areas were left uncovered.
This policy is
   A. *undesirable*; overlap is frequently necessary
   B. *desirable*; the presence of overlap and duplication indicates defective planning
   C. *undesirable*; setting up general policy in advance of the specific reporting system may lead to inflexibility
   D. *desirable*; it is not necessary to get complete coverage in order to be able to plan operations
   E. *undesirable*; duplication is preferable to leaving any area uncovered

Questions 13-15.

DIRECTIONS: Questions 13 through 15 are to be answered on the basis of the following paragraph.

Prior to revising its child care program, a department feels that it is necessary to get some information from the mothers served by the existing program in order to determine where changes are required. A questionnaire is to be constructed to obtain this information.

13. Of the following points which can be taken into consideration in the construction of the questionnaire, the one which is of LEAST importance is
    A. that the data are to be put into punch cards
    B. the aspects of the program which seem to be in need of change
    C. the type of person who will fill out the questionnaire
    D. testing the questionnaire for ambiguity in advance of general distribution
    E. setting up a control group so that answers received can be compared to a standard

13.____

14. To discuss this questionnaire with all mothers who have been asked to answer it, before they actually fill it out, is
    A. *desirable*; the mothers may be able to offer valuable suggestions for changes in the form of the questionnaire
    B. *undesirable*; it is of some value but consumes too much valuable time
    C. *desirable*; cooperation and uniform interpretation will tend to be achieved
    D. *undesirable*; it may cause the answers to be biased
    E. *desirable*; the group will tend to support the program

14.____

15. Of the following items included in the questionnaire, the one which will be of LEAST assistance for comparing attitudes toward the program among different kinds of persons is
    A. name   B. address
    C. age   D. place of birth
    E. education

15.____

16. You have been asked, to prepare for public distribution, a statement dealing with a controversial matter.
    Of the following approaches, the one which would usually be MOST effective is to present your department's point of view
    A. as tersely as possible with no reference to any other matters
    B. developed from ideas and facts well known to most readers
    C. and show all the statistical data and techniques which were used in arriving at it
    D. in such a way that the controversial parts are omitted
    E. substantiated by supporting quotations from persons in the specialized field even if they are not well known

16.____

5 (#2)

17. During a conference of administrative staff personnel, the department head discussing the letter prepared for his signature stated, *"Use no more words than are necessary to express your meaning."*
Following this rule in letter writing is, in general,
   A. *desirable*; considerable time will be saved in the preparation of correspondence
   B. *undesirable*; it is frequently necessary to elaborate on an explanation in order to make certain that the reader will understand
   C. *desirable*; terse statements give government letters a business-like air which impresses readers favorably
   D. *undesirable*; terse statements are generally cold and formal and produce an unfavorable reaction in the reader
   E. *desirable*; the use of more words than are necessary is likely to obscure the meaning and tire the reader

17.____

18. While you are designing the layout for a departmental procedure manual, it is suggested that you carefully arrange your reading material so that there will be a minimum amount of blank space on the page.
Of the following judgments of this suggestion, the one which is the MOST valid basis for action is that it is
   A. *bad*; readability and ease of reference will be decreased
   B. *good*; the cost of production can be decreased considerably without any great disadvantage
   C. *of little or no importance*; more or less blank space on the page will not affect the value of the manual
   D. *good*; it will make for a smaller, easier to handle book
   E. *bad*; replacement of outdated pages is made more difficult by having more material on a page

18.____

19. After the planning of an employee's procedure manual had been completed, the suggestion was made that the manual should be prepared and arranged so that changes could be made readily.
Of the following decisions with respect to this suggestion, the one which is MOST desirable from the viewpoint of good administration is that the suggestions should
   A. not be considered as it is generally impossible to prepare a satisfactory manual which will take everything into consideration
   B. be followed only if it does not conflict with the planned layout
   C. be used even if it is somewhat more costly than the planned layout
   D. be noted and acted upon at the next revision of the manual
   E. not be considered as this type of manual is more difficult to maintain properly

19.____

20. Assume that you are in charge of preparing a procedure manual of about 100 pages for a large clerical unit. After you have decided to use a looseleaf format, one of your subordinates proposes that only one side of the page be printed.

20.____

This proposal is
- A. *good*; replacement of obsolete pages is made easier
- B. *poor*; cost is increased
- C. *good*; provision is automatically made for employee's notes
- D. *poor*; it will increase the size of the manual, making it more difficult to use
- E *good*; indexing will be made easier

21. It may be assumed that if all departments had qualified personnel officers, not all departments would be lacking adequate training programs. However, the most cursory examination of the situation will show that some departments do not have adequate training programs. Thus, we must conclude that some of them lack qualified personnel officers.
The argument presented in the report is
    - A. *correct*; the conclusion follows logically from the assumption and the facts
    - B. *not correct*; what can be concluded is that no department has a qualified personnel officer
    - C. *not correct*; no conclusion with respect to the presence of personnel officers in departments can be drawn from the information
    - D. *not correct*; what can be concluded is that the absence of an adequate training program in a department implies the absence of a personnel officer
    - E. *correct*; but the conclusion is false as the hypothesis is not true

22. In a study of the relationship between a fixed discipline policy and the incidence of lateness, it would be MOST informative to have data proving the statement:
    - A. In those organizations in which there are no fixed discipline policy, the incidence of lateness is variable.
    - B. The incidence of lateness has not decreased in those organizations where fixed discipline policies have been abandoned.
    - C. The incidence of lateness and the discipline policy vary from organization to organization.
    - D. Discipline policies sometimes ignore the problem of lateness.
    - E. In organizations with a fixed discipline policy, the incidence of lateness is variable.

23. The data prove that an increase in the number of clerks performing filing work results in an increased cost per item filed.
On the basis of these data, we can be certain that
    - A. if filing costs per item filed increase, it is caused by an increase in the number of clerks filing
    - B. if filing costs per item filed decrease, the number of clerks filing cannot be increasing
    - C. if the number of clerks filing is changed, the unit cost per filing will change
    - D. if the number of clerks filing is not increased, the cost per unit filed will not increase
    - E. if the number of clerks filing is decreased, the cost per item filed will decrease

7 (#2)

24. Each unit either has sufficient space assigned to it or it has not. No unit which has insufficient space assigned to it has neglected to ask for additional space. From these data, we can state
    A. units with sufficient space have not asked for additional space
    B. only units which have sufficient space have not asked for additional space
    C. nothing about the relationship between the need for additional space and requests made for additional space
    D. all units which have requested additional space have insufficient space
    E. no units which have requested additional space have sufficient space

24.____

25. One argument which is presented against a strict career system in the civil service is as follows:
    The employees who are recruited today for low-level jobs become the administrators of tomorrow. At the present time the employees we are attracting for the low-level jobs are untrained and poorly educated. Thus, it follows that the administrators of tomorrow will be untrained and poorly educated.
    The one of the following which is a CORRECT criticism of the reasoning is that
    A. the argument is logically correct but the conclusion is false as the hypothesis that we are attracting untrained and poorly educated people for our low-level job is false
    B. the conclusion does not follow logically from hypotheses
    C. the argument is logically correct, but the conclusion is false because it is a false hypothesis that tomorrow's administrators will come from employees who hold low-level jobs
    D. the argument is logically correct and the conclusion is correct
    E. while the argument is logically correct and the hypotheses are not demonstrably false, the argument ignores the realities of the case that those who are untrained today may be trained tomorrow

25.____

KEY (CORRECT ANSWERS)

1.	B	11.	C
2.	D	12.	E
3.	E	13.	E
4.	E	14.	C
5.	A	15.	A
6.	B	16.	B
7.	E	17.	E
8.	C	18.	A
9.	D	19.	C
10.	D	20.	A

21.	C
22.	B
23.	B
24.	B
25.	B

TEST 3

DIRECTIONS: Each question or incomplete statement is followed by several suggested answers or completions. Select the one that BEST answers the question or completes the statement. *PRINT THE LETTER OF THE CORRECT ANSWER IN THE SPACE AT THE RIGHT.*

1. Surveying modern administration, it becomes clear that there is GREATEST need at present for administrators with
   A. a good knowledge of personnel administration
   B. the ability to write good reports
   C. a working knowledge of modern methods analysis
   D. a broad rather than specialized viewpoint
   E. the ability to analyze complicated fiscal programs

   1.____

2. The one of the following which is a fundamental obstacle to effective planning in MOST governmental agencies is
   A. inadequate staff or resources
   B. the absence of the properly centralized administration
   C. the absence of clearly defined objective and constituent programs
   D. the neglect of analysis of ways and means
   E. the absence of functional boundaries for units and individuals

   2.____

3. A department consists of several independent bureaus, each responsible to the commissioner for its own planning, operation, and reporting, a central personnel unit and the commissioner's office consisting of a secretary and several clerks to handle public relations.
   The one of the following *undesirable* characteristics which is MOST likely to arise in this organization is
   A. absence of planning
   B. weak and ineffectual leadership
   C. failure to have employees properly trained
   D. a lack of an easily understandable goal
   E. duplication of work

   3.____

4. The one of the following practices which is MOST likely to lead to confusion, recrimination and jurisdictional conflict among the bureaus of a department is the failure to
   A. make clear and unambiguous assignments
   B. systematically subdivide the work
   C. explain general policy to those responsible for its achievement
   D. allocate equitably available resources
   E. set up uniform operating procedures for all units

   4.____

5. The one of the following which is MOST likely to occur in an over-specialized administrative set-up is
   A. inability to recruit proper personnel to fill over-specialized positions
   B. improper supervision
   C. failure of employees to realize the broad implications of their work

   5.____

D. lack of proper decentralization of authority, as emphasis on specialization goes hand-in-hand with over-centralization
E. inability to solve technical problems which are not entirely in one specialty

6. Of the following, the LEAST valid reason for a department head continuing to require that a weekly report be forwarded to him, is that the report forms a basis for
   A. measuring performance
   B. making decisions
   C. revising policy
   D. the execution of the mission of the unit which receives it
   E. the operation of the unit which is required to prepare it

7. Administrators must learn not to farm out essential functions to unintegrated agencies, but to organize all responsibilities in unified but decentralized hierarchies.
   A problem which an administrator may be expected to face if he has not learned this is that
   A. the organization fails to develop administrators capable of independent action
   B. issues will not be posed at the level where decisions should be made
   C. relationships with the public will not be satisfactory
   D. it will be difficult to achieve administrative control or get agreement on departmental action
   E. individual agencies will be unable to complete the work scheduled

8. The central staff planning unit within any organization includes in its functions helping to plan policy at one extreme and planning detailed execution at the other extreme.
   With respect to the actual execution, the planning activity should
   A. have no concern with it
   B. simply forward and explain new plans
   C. have only the responsibility of explaining in the form of plans the objectives of top management
   D. keep track of how the plans are working out but make no attempt to supervise their execution
   E. supervise the execution of new plans

9. The head of a department assigned final responsibility for the training function to the personnel office.
   This assignment was
   A. *undesirable*; this type of centralization prevents a staff organization from carrying out staff functions
   B. *desirable*; experience has shown that centralization of this type results in more efficient and economic operation
   C. *undesirable*; the personnel office usually does not have the technical "know how" to carry this responsibility
   D. *desirable*; if training is left to the line officials, it never is accomplished
   E. *undesirable*; this responsibility must rest with the supervisor

10. A department head insisted that operating officials participate in the development of new procedures along with the planning section.
    Participation of this type is, on the whole,
    A. *desirable*; operating realities are more likely to be considered
    B. *undesirable*; the inclusion of conflicting views before the plan is drawn may result in no plan
    C. *desirable*; plans will be more flexible and objectives more clearly defined
    D. *undesirable*; the operating officials should decide to what extent they wish to participate with no pressure from the top
    E. *desirable*; to back down on a procedure once it has been decided upon is a sign of weakness

11. Much of the current criticism of the administration of large organizations is basically a criticism of our failure to place the same emphasis on accountability that we do on authority and responsibility.
    The one of the following acts which is MOST likely to insure accountability for the discharge of responsibilities inherent in the delegation of authority is the
    A. establishment of appropriate reports and controls
    B. organization of a methods analysis section
    C. delegation of authority so made as to support functional or homogeneous activities
    D. delegation of authority so made as to preserve unity of command
    E. decentralization of responsibility and authority

12. This statement has been made:
    A man who is a top-notch executive in one organization would make a top-notch executive in any other organization, even if the organizations are as diverse as a sales agency and a research foundation.
    This statement is, in general,
    A. *correct*; the characteristics required for a good executive are invariant with respect to organization
    B. *incorrect*; there is no way of predicting how a good executive in one organization would be in any other
    C. *correct*; while the characteristics required for a good executive vary from organization to organization, the common core requirements are great enough to insure similar performance
    D. *incorrect*; although some prediction can be made, different types of organizations require different types of executives
    E. *correct*; success as an executive does not depend upon "characteristics" but on the man; if he is able to direct and execute in one organization he will be able to do so in any other

13. Reported information is not needed at levels higher than those at which decisions are made on the basis of the information reported.
    This statement is, in general,
    A. *correct*; if no action is to be taken on the basis of the information, the information is unnecessary
    B. *incorrect*; all information is of importance in arriving at a sound decision

C. *correct*; levels below the one at which the decision is made have need of the information
D. *incorrect*; levels below the one at which the decision is made do not have need of the information
E. *correct*; decisions should be made on the basis of information reported

14. Of the following, the characteristic of an organization which BEST shows that the organizational hierarchy is effective is that
    A. the department head commands the respect of the employees
    B. the organization is sufficiently flexible to assume functions in fields not related to his major field of endeavor
    C. responsibility has been appropriately delegated throughout the organization
    D. the department continues to function effectively even though there is continual turnover in the higher supervisory ranks
    E. no employee in the organization is subject to orders from more than one source

15. It is only because the primary purpose of traditional discipline has been to preserve the structure of command that a need has arisen for ameliorative safeguards such as a formal statement of "cause," right of hearing, and right of appeal.
    The BEST current practice with respect to discipline is that
    A. few ameliorative safeguards of the kind enumerated are desirable as their presence hurts the public service
    B. discipline is a means of controlling deviations from established authority
    C. the safeguards enumerated are not sufficient for the protection of the employee
    D. discipline should be based upon education, persuasion, and consultation
    E. unquestioned obedience to each order should not be expected but that a supervisor should be prepared at all times to demonstrate the reasonableness of his requests

16. Of the following types of work, the one for which a manual process is MOST usually to be preferred over a mechanized process is one in which the transactions are very
    A. numerous   B. similar   C. dissimilar
    D. predictable   E. unpredictable

17. Work flow charts are used in an organization PRIMARILY because they
    A. indicate present and future objectives clearly
    B. are frequently used records
    C. clearly indicate when each operation will be performed
    D. summarize the work procedures of the organization
    E. tend to clarify thinking by presenting certain facts clearly

5 (#3)

18. With respect to a report prepared by an IBM installation, the one of the following changes which is LEAST likely to cause a change in the procedure for preparing the report is a change in the
    A. volume of work
    B. source documents
    C. final report
    D. employees assigned
    E. time allowed for the preparation of the report

    18.____

19. The one of the following which is NOT necessarily a characteristic of a good buying procedure is that it
    A. provides for proper analysis of purchases made
    B. is simple
    C. makes provision for substitutions where possible and necessary
    D. makes sealed bids mandatory
    E. recruits many bidders

    19.____

20. Data relating to the operation of any unit should be accumulated and periodically summarized and analyzed PRIMARILY in order to
    A. point out the most efficient and least efficient workers
    B. determine the relative value of each procedure
    C. locate the elements of an operation which are unusually efficient or inefficient
    D. evaluate the importance of maintaining operating records and quotas
    E. compare the work performed by comparable units

    20.____

21. Of the following, the MAJOR function of an administrative planning and research staff units is to
    A. investigate trouble points in the organization
    B. reorganize inefficient units
    C. assist the executive to plan future operations
    D. conduct continuous investigations and planning
    E. write the necessary operation and procedure manuals

    21.____

22. The one of the following which does NOT require definition when setting up a work measurement system is the
    A. level of work accomplishment at which to measure
    B. work unit in which to measure
    C. time unit by which to measure
    D. acceptable quota for each activity
    E. reporting system to be used

    22.____

23. During a discussion of the time unit that would be appropriate to measure employee-time in a work measurement program in a public agency, the man-day was suggested.
    This unit is
    A. *satisfactory*; record keeping will be kept to a minimum
    B. *unsatisfactory*; it will be difficult to verify the unit against official time records

    23.____

C. *satisfactory*; it will be easy to verify the unit against official time records
D. *unsatisfactory*; its use will unnecessarily complicate record keeping
E. *satisfactory*; it permits more meaningful comparisons to be made between equal periods of time

24. As part of a space layout survey, an administrator instructed his subordinates to study the flow of work and sequence of operating procedures.
His MAJOR purposes in doing this was to determine
    A. the physical distribution and movement of personnel, material, and equipment
    B. the amount of space which is available and the amount of space which will be required
    C. the order in which the component steps in the different procedures are performed
    D. what future requirements will be, based on observable present trend
    E. how the distribution of personnel to various organization units is related to their space requirements

25. Before discussing a proposed office layout, the administrative officer stated, *"We intend to have a minimum number of private offices. We will assign private offices only where quiet is deemed essential or confidential conferences are required."*
The one of the following which is usually the MOST valid reason for this rule is that it
    A. permits proper placing of employees who deal with the public
    B. makes it easier to locate supervisors near the units they control
    C. tends to ensure that the work of each unit will flow continually forward within itself
    D. allows placing complementary units close together
    E. makes clerical supervision easier

KEY (CORRECT ANSWERS)

1.	D	11.	A
2.	C	12.	D
3.	E	13.	A
4.	A	14.	C
5.	C	15.	D
6.	E	16.	C
7.	D	17.	E
8.	D	18.	D
9.	E	19.	D
10.	A	20.	C

21.	D
22.	D
23.	D
24.	A
25.	E

EXAMINATION SECTION
TEST 1

DIRECTIONS: Each question or incomplete statement is followed by several suggested answers or completions. Select the one that BEST answers the question or completes the statement. *PRINT THE LETTER OF THE CORRECT ANSWER IN THE SPACE AT THE RIGHT.*

1. Assume that a two story building measures 21'6" x 53'7". It is in a district that calls for an open space ratio of .80. The required open space on this lot must be *most nearly* square feet.

    A. 922   B. 1152   C. 1843   D. 2880

    1.____

2. Assume that the elevation at the back of a lot is 127.36 ft. and the elevation at the front of the same lot is 125.49 ft.
The difference in elevation between front and back of the lot is *most nearly*

    A. 1'10 1/8"   B. 1'10 1/4"   C. 1'10 3/8"   D. 1'10 1/2"

    2.____

3. The sketch below represents the lowest story of a new building. In order for this story to be considered a basement, the elevation of the first floor must be AT LEAST

    A. 131.09   B. 131.14   C. 131.19   D. 131.24

    3.____

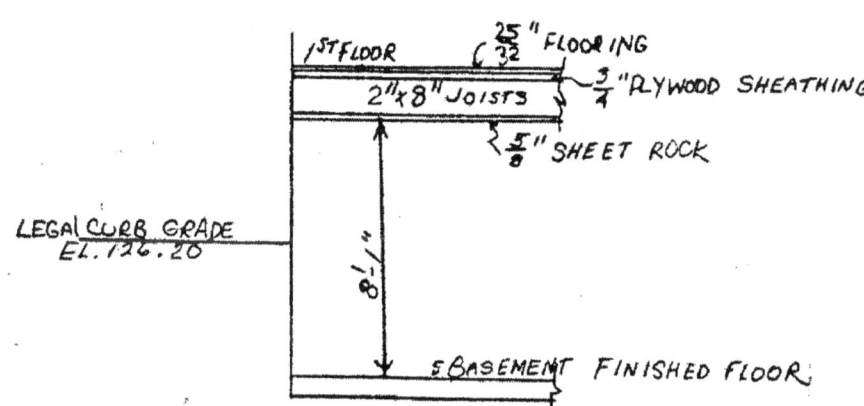

4. The MOST important requirement of a good report is that it should be

    A. properly addressed   B. clear and concise
    C. verbose   D. spelled correctly

    4.____

5. Of the following, in determining whether a violation should be referred for court action, the MOST important item that should be considered is

    A. the amount of available time you have to process the case
    B. the availability of the inspector
    C. whether or not the owner has indicated a desire to cooperate with the department
    D. whether or not the case is important enough to warrant court action

    5.____

6. In the Zoning Resolution, the size of required side yards would be found in the chapters on

    A. Use Groups
    B. Bulk Regulations
    C. Area Districts
    D. District Boundaries

    6.___

7. According to the Zoning Resolution, the one of the following that is NOT considered part of the floor area of a building is a(n)

    A. basement
    B. stairwell at floor level
    C. penthouse
    D. attached garage on 1st floor

    7.___

8. The one of the following that is permitted by the Zoning Resolution as a home occupation is

    A. veterinary medicine
    B. real estate broker
    C. teaching of music
    D. public relations agency

    8.___

9. For the purpose of determining the number of rooms in a dwelling unit, the Zoning Resolution adds an arbitrary number to the number of *living rooms*.
   Where there are six or less living rooms, this arbitrary number is

    A. 1/2   B. 1   C. 1 1/2   D. 2

    9.___

10. Assuming the following signs are all 10 square feet in area, the one that is NOT subject to the provisions of the Zoning Resolution is one indicating

    A. a freight entrance to a building
    B. a fund drive for a civic organization
    C. vacancies in an apartment building
    D. a parking area at the rear of a structure

    10.___

11. On a plan, the symbol ~~~~~ represents

    A. earth
    B. wood
    C. metal lath
    D. marble

    11.___

12. On a plan, the symbol represents

    A. cinder
    B. brick
    C. plywood
    D. rock lath and plaster

    12.___

13. On a plan, the symbol represents

    A. glass
    B. asphalt shingles
    C. concrete
    D. porcelain enamel

    13.___

14. A corbel is a form of

    A. cricket B. crown molding
    C. cantilever D. curtain wall

15. In balloon type framing, the second floor joists rest on a

    A. sole plate B. ribband
    C. header D. sill

16. Condensation of moisture in inadequately ventilated attics or roof spaces is usually GREATEST in

    A. summer B. autumn C. winter D. spring

17. Of the following combinations of tread and riser, the one that would be acceptable for required stairs in either a new office building or a multiple dwelling is

    A. 9 1/4", 7 1/2" B. 9 1/2", 7 1/4"
    C. 9 1/2", 7 3/4" D. 10", 8"

18. A meeting rail is a common part of a

    A. door frame B. window sash
    C. stairwell D. bulkhead

19. If doors in an old building do not close, it is MOST probably an indication that the

    A. frames have shrunk
    B. building has settled
    C. hinges were not set properly
    D. wood used for the doors are of inferior grade

20. Cracks in concrete are not necessarily caused by settlement of a structure. Sometimes they are caused by

    A. shrinkage B. curing
    C. hydration D. over-troweling

KEY (CORRECT ANSWERS)

1. C
2. D
3. A
4. B
5. C

6. B
7. D
8. C
9. C
10. B

11. A
12. B
13. A
14. C
15. B

16. C
17. C
18. B
19. B
20. A

TEST 2

DIRECTIONS: Each question or incomplete statement is followed by several suggested answers or completions. Select the one that BEST answers the question or completes the statement. *PRINT THE LETTER OF THE CORRECT ANSWER IN THE SPACE AT THE RIGHT.*

1. Required exit doors from a room must open in the direction of egress when the room is occupied by more than _____ persons. 1.____
   A. 15 B. 25 C. 35 D. 50

2. A window in a masonry wall on a lot line 2.____
   A. is not permitted
   B. must have a fire resistive rating of 3/4 hour
   C. must have a fire resistive rating of 1 hour
   D. must have a fire resistive rating of 1 1/2 hours

3. Air entrained concrete is required in all cases for 3.____
   A. garage floors   B. footings
   C. grade beams   D. columns

4. A parapet wall or railing would be required on new non-residential structures where the height of the structure is greater than (give lowest height specified by law) _____ feet. 4.____
   A. 15 B. 19 C. 22 D. 25

5. Of the following statements, the one that is CORRECT is that wood joists may 5.____
   A. not be supported on a fire wall
   B. be supported on a fire wall only if fireproofed wall is used
   C. be supported on a fire wall only if they are separated from each other by at least 4 inches of solid masonry
   D. be supported on a fire wall only if they are separated from each other by at least 12 inches of solid masonry

6. A foundation wall below grade may be of hollow block only if the building 6.____
   A. is a residence
   B. is no more than one story high
   C. is of frame construction
   D. has no cellar or basement

7. The Building Code specifies that lintels are required to be fire-proofed when the opening is more than _____ feet. 7.____
   A. 3 B. 4 C. 5 D. 6

8. In a 12-inch brick wall, the MAXIMUM permitted depth of a chase is 8.____
   A. none B. 4" C. 6" D. 8"

9. Wood joists should clear flues and chimneys by at least 9.____
   A. 1" B. 2" C. 3" D. 4"

10. Fire retarding or enclosure in shafts of all vent ducts are required when they   10.____

    A. go through more than one floor
    B. are used for intake as well as exhaust
    C. are more than 144 square inches in area
    D. are in rooms subdivided with wood partitions

11. Assume a builder is unable to complete the pour for a continuous concrete floor slab. The   11.____
    slab is supported by beams and girders.
    The construction joint should be made at a point

    A. over a beam
    B. one quarter of the span length from the beam
    C. one third of the span length from the beam
    D. midway between beams

12. Under required stairs in a Class 3 building,   12.____

    A. it is unlawful to locate a closet
    B. a closet is permitted provided that the stringers are fire retarded
    C. a closet is permitted provided that the closet is completely lined with incombustible material
    D. a closet is permitted provided that fireproof wood is used to frame out the closet

13. In New York City, the exit provisions of the State Labor Law apply   13.____

    A. only to factories
    B. to factories and warehouses
    C. to factories, warehouses, and restaurants
    D. to all types of uses

14. A Class 3 building, two stories high, may have required stairs enclosed with stud parti-   14.____
    tions fire retarded with gypsum boards unless the building is used for a

    A. factory   B. storage warehouse
    C. bowling alley   D. department store

15. The one of the following rooms in a *place of assembly* that is required to be sprinklered is   15.____
    a

    A. performer's dressing room
    B. kitchen
    C. service pantry
    D. waiting room

16. Of the following, the FIRST operation in the demolition of a building is the   16.____

    A. shoring of the adjoining buildings
    B. erection of railings around stairwells
    C. removal of windows
    D. venting of the roof

17. As used in the Building Code, *consistency* of concrete refers to   17.____

    A. composition   B. water-cement ratio
    C. relative plasticity   D. proportion of aggregates

18. One condition that is required for a building to be considered a *Special Occupancy Structure* is that the building is used for 18.____

    A. a theater
    B. a church
    C. a restaurant
    D. motor vehicle repairs

19. A wire glass vision panel on a door opening into a fire tower is 19.____

    A. not permitted
    B. permitted if the panel has a fire rating of 3/4 hour
    C. permitted if the panel has a fire rating of 3/4 hour and is less than 100 square inches in area
    D. permitted if the panel has a fire rating of 3/4 hour, is less than 100 square inches in area, and is glazed with two thicknesses of wire glass with an air space between

20. One of the requirements that must be met before untreated wood can be used as a subdividing partition in a Class 1 building is that the partition 20.____

    A. be no more than 8 feet high
    B. enclose an area less than 200 square feet in size
    C. enclose office space only
    D. be made of a single thickness of wood

KEY (CORRECT ANSWERS)

1.	D	11.	D
2.	B	12.	C
3.	A	13.	A
4.	C	14.	C
5.	C	15.	A
6.	D	16.	C
7.	B	17.	C
8.	B	18.	A
9.	D	19.	A
10.	A	20.	D

TEST 3

DIRECTIONS: Each question or incomplete statement is followed by several suggested answers or completions. Select the one that BEST answers the question or completes the statement. *PRINT THE LETTER OF THE CORRECT ANSWER IN THE SPACE AT THE RIGHT.*

1. There are two criteria required for determining whether a multiple dwelling shall be classified as a *converted dwelling*.
The FIRST is the number of families originally occupying the dwelling, and the second is the

   A. conjunctive uses
   B. date of erection of the building
   C. classification, whether Class A or B
   D. number of families now occupying the dwelling

2. According to the Multiple Dwelling Law, a *dinette* is NOT considered a living room if its area is _____ sq. ft. or less.

   A. 50   B. 55   C. 59   D. 64

3. Where a building faces only one street, the curb level used for measuring the height of the building is the

   A. lowest curb level in front of the building
   B. highest curb level in front of the building
   C. level of the curb at the center of the front of the building
   D. average of the levels of the lowest and highest curb level in front of the building

4. According to the Multiple Dwelling Code, one of the living rooms in each apartment of a newly created multiple dwelling shall have a MINIMUM floor area of _____ square feet.

   A. 59   B. 110   C. 150   D. 175

5. It is proposed to alter an old law tenement so as to increase the number of apartments. Of the following, the one that MOST completely gives the requirements to be met before the alteration can be approved is: Each new apartment must be provided a

   A. water closet
   B. water closet and a wash basin
   C. water closet, a wash basin, and a bath or shower
   D. water closet, a wash basin, a bath or shower, and centrally supplied heat

6. Gas fueled space heaters may be permitted in lieu of centrally supplied heat.
One of the following conditions required before the use of space heaters can be permitted is that

   A. each apartment has no more than two living rooms
   B. the building is a Class A multiple dwelling
   C. all apartments are used for single room occupancy
   D. D, the gas line supplying the heater be connected directly to the main so that the tenant cannot control the flow of gas

7. An incinerator is required in all multiple

   A. dwellings
   B. dwellings four or more stories in height
   C. dwellings four or more stories in height and occupied by more than twelve families
   D. dwellings four or more stories in height occupied by more than twelve families and erected after October 1, 1951

8. Tests of required sprinkler systems in a single room occupancy building must be made

   A. monthly
   B. quarterly
   C. semi-annually
   D. annually

9. An additional apartment may be created on the first floor of a Class A frame converted dwelling provided that no more than two families will occupy this floor and

   A. the entrance hall is sprinklered
   B. the building is brick veneered
   C. there is no basement occupancy
   D. all stairs are enclosed in one hour fire partitions

10. The MAIN feature differentiating a *five tower* from a *fire stair* is the

    A. fire rating of the enclosure walls
    B. use to which the fire tower is put
    C. method of entering the fire tower from the building
    D. height of the fire tower

11. A new elevator shaft is to be built into a non-fireproof multiple dwelling. Of the following materials, the one that has the lowest fire resistance that would be acceptable for the enclosure walls of this shaft is

    A. 3" solid gypsum block
    B. 2" x 4" studs with 5/8" fire code 60 each side
    C. steel studs, wire mesh and 3/4" P.C. plaster
    D. 4" hollow concrete blocks, plastered both sides

12. Of the following statements, the one that is MOST complete and accurate is that a frame extension 70 sq. ft. in area added to a frame multiple dwelling is

    A. not permitted
    B. permitted only if the walls of the extension are brick filled
    C. permitted only if the walls of the extension are brick filled and the extension is to be used solely for bathrooms
    D. permitted only if the walls of the extension are brick filled, the extension is to be used solely for bathrooms and the walls are at least 3 ft. from the side lot lines

13. Assume it is proposed to extend a business use in a non-fireproof multiple dwelling by erecting an extension at the rear of the building. The roof the extension is required to be fireproof

    A. in all cases
    B. when the business use requires a combustible occupancy permit
    C. when there are fire escapes above the extension
    D. if the business use is a factory

14. In a Class A dwelling, two water closets may 14.____

    A. be placed in one compartment only in old law tenements
    B. be placed in one compartment in either old law or new law tenements
    C. be placed in one compartment in all types of apartment houses
    D. not be placed in one compartment

15. According to the Multiple Dwelling Law, a janitor is NOT required when the maximum 15.____
    number of families occupying the dwelling is

    A. 6   B. 9   C. 12   D. 15

16. The first floor above the lowest cellar in a non-fireproof multiple dwelling does NOT have 16.____
    to be fireproof if

    A. the cellar is used only for incombustible storage
    B. there are two means of egress from the cellar
    C. the building is no more than three stories in height
    D. the dwelling is occupied by no more than nine families

17. In a converted multiple dwelling, ventilation of a room on the top story may be obtained 17.____
    by

    A. a skylight
    B. a duct with a wind blown hood
    C. a duct with an electrically operated fan
    D. by a window only and no other method is acceptable

18. *It* is proposed to build a closet under the stairs leading to the second floor in a non-fire- 18.____
    proof *new law* tenement. This is

    A. not permitted
    B. permitted only if the entire closet is built of non-combustible materials
    C. permitted only if the closet is used for non-combustible storage
    D. permitted if the closet is built of fire-retarded partitions and the soffit of the stairs is
       also fire-retarded

19. For multiple dwellings erected after April 18, 1929, a ladder from a fire escape to a roof is 19.____
    NOT required when

    A. the building is three stories or less in height
    B. the roof is built of incombustible material
    C. the fire escape is on the front of the building
    D. there is no safe access from the roof to another building

20. It is proposed to convert a Class B multiple dwelling used for summer resort occupancy 20.____
    to year-round Class B use. This conversion is

    A. illegal
    B. legal provided the exits comply with the requirements for Class B use
    C. legal provided the exits and toilet facilities comply with the requirements for Class
       B use
    D. legal provided the exits, toilet facilities, and ventilation requirements comply with
       the requirements for Class B use

KEY (CORRECT ANSWERS)

1. B
2. B
3. C
4. C
5. D

6. B
7. D
8. D
9. B
10. C

11. A
12. A
13. C
14. A
15. C

16. C
17. A
18. A
19. C
20. A

DOCUMENTS AND FORMS
PREPARING WRITTEN MATERIALS
EXAMINATION SECTION
TEST 1

DIRECTIONS: Each question or incomplete statement is followed by several suggested answers or completions. Select the one that BEST answers the question or completes the statement. *PRINT THE LETTER OF THE CORRECT ANSWER IN THE SPACE AT THE RIGHT.*

1. The office layout chart is a sketch of the physical arrangement of the office to which has been added the flow lines of the principal work performed there.
   Which one of the following states the BEST advantage of superimposing the work flow onto the desk layout?

   A. Lighting and acoustics can be improved.
   B. Line and staff relationships can be determined.
   C. Obvious misarrangements can be corrected.
   D. The number of delays can be determined.

   1.____

2. An advantage of the multiple process chart over the flow process chart is that the multiple process chart shows the

   A. individual worker's activity
   B. number of delays
   C. sequence of operations
   D. simultaneous flow of work in several departments

   2.____

3. Of the following, which is the MAJOR advantage of a microfilm record retention system?

   A. Filing can follow the terminal digit system.
   B. Retrieving documents from the files is faster.
   C. Significant space is saved in storing records.
   D. To read a microfilm record, a film reader is not necessary.

   3.____

4. Assume that you are in the process of eliminating unnecessary forms.
   The answer to which one of the following questions would be LEAST relevant?

   A. Could the information be obtained elsewhere?
   B. Is the form properly designed?
   C. Is the form used as intended?
   D. Is the purpose of the form essential to the operation?

   4.____

5. Use of color in forms adds to their cost. Sometimes, however, the use of color will greatly simplify procedure and more than pay for itself in time saved and errors eliminated.
   This is ESPECIALLY true when

   A. a form passes through many reviewers
   B. considerable sorting is required
   C. the form is other than a standard size
   D. the form will not be sent through the mail

   5.____

6. Of the following techniques, the one *generally* employed and considered BEST in forms design is to provide writing lines into boxes with captions printed in small type

    A. centered in the lower part of the box
    B. centered in the upper part of the box
    C. in the upper left-hand corner of the box
    D. in the lower right-hand corner of the box

7. Many forms authorities advocate the construction of a functional forms file or index. If such a file is set up, the MOST effective way of classifying forms for such an index is classification by

    A. department
    B. form number
    C. name or type of form
    D. subject to which the form applies

8. Of the following, the symbol as used in a systems flow chart denotes
    A. decision
    B. document
    C. manual operation
    D. process

9. Assume you are assigned to analyze the details of the procedures a clerk follows in order to complete filling out an invoice or a requisition. Your purpose is to simplify and shorten the procedure he has been trained to use.
    The BEST appropriate chart for this purpose would be the

    A. block flow diagram   B. flow process chart
    C. forms flow chart   D. work distribution chart

10. What *generally* is the PRINCIPAL objection to the use of form letters? The

    A. difficulty of developing a form letter to serve the purpose
    B. excessive time involved in selecting the proper form letter
    C. errors in selecting form letters
    D. impersonality of form letters

11. In process charting, the symbol which is used when conditions (except those which intentionally change the physical or chemical characteristics of the object) do not permit or require immediate performance, is

    A. □   B. ○   C. D   D. ▽

12. Assume that you are making a study of a central headquarters office which processes claims received from a number of district offices. You notice the following problems: Some employees are usually busy, while others doing the same kind of work in the same grade have little to do; high level professional people frequently spend considerable time searching for files in the file room. Which of the following charts would be MOST useful to record and analyze the data needed to help solve these problems? 12.____

    A. Forms distribution chart
    B. Process chart
    C. Space layout chart
    D. Work distribution chart

13. Which of the following questions has the LEAST significant bearing on the analysis of the paperwork flow? 13.____

    A. How is the work brought into the department and how is it taken away?
    B. How many work stations are involved in processing the work within the department?
    C. Is the work received and removed in the proper quantity?
    D. Where is the supervisor's desk located in relationship to those he supervises?

14. Which of the following does NOT have significant bearing on the arrangement, sequence, and zoning of information into box captions? The 14.____

    A. layout of the source documents from which the information is taken
    B. logical flow of data
    C. needs of forms to be prepared from this form
    D. type of print to be employed

15. In determining the space requirements of a form and the size of the boxes to be used, PRIMARY consideration should be given to the 15.____

    A. distribution of the form
    B. method of entry, i.e., handwritten or machine, and type of machine
    C. number of copies
    D. number of items to be entered

16. Of the following, the BEST technique to follow when providing instructions for the completion and routing of a form is to 16.____

    A. imprint the instructions on the face of the form
    B. imprint the instructions on the back of the form
    C. provide a written procedure to accompany the form
    D. provide verbal instructions when issuing the form

17. A forms layout style where a separate space in the shape of a box is provided for each item of information requested and the caption or question for each item is shown in the upper left-hand corner of each box, is known as the 17.____

    A. box style
    B. check box style
    C. check list style
    D. check box and check list style

18. The BEST type of chart to use in showing the absolute movement or change of a continuous series of data over a period of time, such as changes in prices, employment or expenses, is *usually* a 18.____

A. bar chart B. line chart
C. multiple bar chart D. pie chart

19. In order to secure information on several specific points from all the tenants of a project, it has been suggested that a questionnaire be distributed to be completed and returned by the tenants.
The use of such a procedure is, *generally,*

    A. *desirable,* because it is a valuable means of building the cooperative relationship which should exist between tenants and management
    B. *desirable,* because it provides a written record of each tenant's reply
    C. *undesirable,* because distribution and collection of questionnaires is time-consuming
    D. *undesirable,* because it makes no provision for the expression of related information or viewpoints

20. A functional forms file is a collection of forms which are grouped by

    A. purpose   B. department   C. title   D. subject

21. All of the following are reasons to consult a records retention schedule EXCEPT one. Which one is that? To determine

    A. whether something should be filed
    B. how long something should stay in file
    C. who should be assigned to filing
    D. when something on file should be destroyed

22. Listed below are four of the steps in the process of preparing correspondence for filing. If they were to be put in logical sequence, the SECOND step would be

    A. preparing cross-reference sheets or cards
    B. coding the correspondence using a classification system
    C. sorting the correspondence in the order to be filed
    D. checking for follow-up action required and preparing a follow-up slip

23. New material added to a file folder should *usually* be inserted

    A. in the order of importance (the most important in front)
    B. in the order of importance (the most important in back)
    C. chronologically (most recent in front)
    D. chronologically (most recent in back)

24. An individual is looking for a name in the white pages of a telephone directory. Which of the following BEST describes the system of filing found there? A(n)

    A. alphabetic file   B. sequential file
    C. locator file   D. index file

25. The MAIN purpose of a tickler file is to

    A. help prevent overlooking matters that require future attention
    B. check on adequacy of past performance
    C. pinpoint responsibility for recurring daily tasks
    D. reduce the volume of material kept in general files

KEY (CORRECT ANSWERS)

1. C
2. D
3. C
4. B
5. B

6. C
7. D
8. A
9. B
10. D

11. C
12. D
13. D
14. D
15. B

16. A
17. A
18. B
19. B
20. A

21. C
22. A
23. C
24. A
25. A

TEST 2

1. A *good* record-keeping system includes all of the following procedures EXCEPT the

    A. filing of useless records
    B. destruction of certain files
    C. transferring of records from one type of file to another
    D. creation of inactive files

2. A new program is being set up for which certain new forms will be needed. You have been asked to design these forms.
   Of the following, the FIRST step you should take in planning the forms is

    A. finding out the exact purpose for which each form will be used
    B. deciding what size of paper should be used for each form
    C. determining whether multiple copies will be needed for any of the forms
    D. setting up a new filing system to handle the new forms

3. Assume that your department is being moved to new and larger quarters, and that you have been asked to suggest an office layout for the central clerical office.
   Of the following, your FIRST step in planning the new layout should *ordinarily* be to

    A. find out how much money has been budgeted for furniture and equipment
    B. make out *work-flow* and *traffic-flow* charts for the clerical operations
    C. measure each piece of furniture and equipment that is presently in use
    D. determine which files should be moved to a storage area or destroyed

4. In modern office layouts, screens and dividers are often used instead of walls to set off working groups. Advantages given for this approach have included *all* of the following EXCEPT

    A. more frequent communication between different working groups
    B. reduction in general noise level
    C. fewer objections from employees who are transferred to different groups
    D. cost savings from increased sharing of office equipment

5. Of the following, the CHIEF reason for moving less active material from active to inactive files is to

    A. dispose of material that no longer has any use
    B. keep the active files down to a manageable size
    C. make sure that no material over a year old remains in active files
    D. separate temporary records from permanent records

6. On a general organization chart, staff positions NORMALLY should be pictured

    A. directly above the line positions to which they report
    B. to the sides of the main flow lines
    C. within the box of the highest level subordinate positions pictured
    D. directly below the line positions which report to them

7. When an administrator is diagramming an office layout, of the following, his PRIMARY job, *generally,* should be to indicate the

   A. lighting intensities that will be required by each operation
   B. noise level that will be produced by the various equipment employed in the office
   C. direction of the work flow and the distance involved in each transfer
   D. durability of major pieces of office equipment currently in use or to be utilized

8. One common guideline or rule-of-thumb ratio for evaluating the efficiency of files is the number of records requested divided by the number of records filed.
   Generally, if this ratio is very low, it would point MOST directly to the need for

   A. improving the indexing and coding system
   B. improving the charge-out procedures
   C. exploring the need for transferring records from active storage to the archives
   D. exploring the need to encourage employees to keep more records in their private files

9. The GREATEST percentage of money spent on preparing and keeping the usual records in an office, *generally,* is expended for which one of the following?

   A. Renting space in which to place the record-keeping equipment
   B. Paying salaries of record-preparing and record-keeping personnel
   C. Depreciation of purchased record-preparation and record-keeping equipment
   D. Paper and forms upon which to place the records

10. The MAXIMUM number of 2 3/4" x 4 1/4" size forms which may be obtained from two reams of 17" x 22" paper is

    A. 4,000   B. 8,000   C. 16,000   D. 32,000

11. Word processing computer applications (i.e. Microsoft Word) generally provide all of the following advantages as compared to electric word processors EXCEPT

    A. documents save to disk automatically
    B. ability to include customized graphs and charts in a document
    C. wider selection of available fonts
    D. easily customized page orientation

12. Generally, the actual floor space occupied by a standard letter-size office file cabinet, when closed, is, *most nearly,*

    A. 1/2 square foot   B. 3 square feet
    C. 7 square feet   D. 11 square feet

13. In general, the CHIEF economy of using multicopy forms is in

    A. the paper on which the form is printed
    B. printing the form
    C. employee time
    D. carbon paper

14. Suppose your supervisor has asked you to develop a form to record certain information needed. The FIRST thing you should do is to

    A. determine the type of data that will be recorded repeatedly, so that it can be pre-printed
    B. study the relationship of the form to the job to be accomplished, so that the form can be planned
    C. determine the information that will be recorded in the same place on each copy of the form, so that it can be used as a check
    D. find out who will be responsible for supplying the information so that space can be provided for their signatures

15. Of the following, which is usually the MOST important guideline in writing business letters? A letter should be

    A. neat
    B. written in a formalized style
    C. written in clear language intelligible to the reader
    D. written in the past tense

16. Suppose you are asked to edit a policy statement. You note that personal pronouns like *you*, *we*, and *I* are used freely.
    Which of the following statements BEST applies to this use of personal pronouns? It

    A. is proper usage because written business language should not be different from carefully spoken business language
    B. requires correction because it is ungrammatical
    C. is proper because it is clearer and has a warmer tone
    D. requires correction because policies should be expressed in an impersonal manner

17. Good business letters are coherent. To be *coherent* means to

    A. keep only one unifying idea in the message
    B. present the total message
    C. use simple, direct words for the message
    D. tie together the various ideas in the message

18. Proper division of a letter into paragraphs requires that the writer of business letters should, as much as possible, be sure that

    A. each paragraph is short
    B. each paragraph develops discussion of just one topic
    C. each paragraph repeats the theme of the total message
    D. there are at least two paragraphs for every message

19. An editor is given a letter with this initial paragraph *We have received your letter, which we read with interest, and we are happy to respond to your question. In fact, we talked with several people in our office to get ideas to send to you.*
    Which of the following is it MOST reasonable for the editor to conclude? The paragraph is

    A. concise B. communicating something of value
    C. unnecessary D. coherent

20. Suppose that one of your duties is to dictate responses to routine requests from the public for information. A letter writer asks for information which, as expressed in a one-sentence, explicit agency rule, cannot be given out to the public.
Of the following ways of answering the letter, which is the MOST efficient?

- A. Quote verbatim that section of the agency rules which prohibits giving this information to the public
- B. Without quoting the rule, explain why you cannot accede to the request and suggest alternative sources
- C. Describe how carefully the request was considered before classifying it as subject to the rule forbidding the issuance of such information
- D. Acknowledge receipt of the letter and advise that the requested information is not released to the public

20.____

21. Suppose you have been asked to write and to prepare for reproduction new departmental vacation leave regulations. After you have written the new regulations, all of which fit on one page, which one of the following would be the BEST method of reproducing 800 copies?

- A. An outside private printer, because you can best maintain confidentiality using this technique
- B. Using your own computer's printer/copier, because it is most convenient
- C. Giving the job to a coworker in another department who does this type of work more frequently, since the coworker is more familiar with the process
- D. Using a high-volume color copier, because it is fastest and of highest quality

21.____

22. The files in your office have been overcrowded and difficult to work with since you started working there. One day your supervisor is transferred and another assistant in your office decides to discard three drawers of the oldest materials.
For him to take this action is

- A. *desirable;* it will facilitate handling the more active materials
- B. *desirable;* no file should be removed from its point of origin
- C. *desirable;* there is no need to burden a new supervisor with unnecessary information
- D. *undesirable;* no file should be discarded without first noting what material has been discarded

22.____

23. You have been criticized by the general supervisor because of spelling errors in some of your typing. You have only copied the reports as written and you realize that the errors occurred in work given to you by your immediate supervisor.
Of the following, the BEST way for you to handle this situation is to

- A. tell the general supervisor that the spelling errors are your immediate supervisor's, not yours, because they occur only when you type his reports
- B. tell the general supervisor that you only type the reports as given to you, without indicating anyone
- C. inform your immediate supervisor that you have been unjustly criticized because of his spelling errors and politely request that he be more careful in the future
- D. use a dictionary whenever you have doubt regarding spelling

23.____

24. You have recently found several items misfiled. You believe that this occurred because a new assistant in your section has been making mistakes.
    The BEST course of action for you to take is to

    A. refile the material and say nothing about it
    B. send your supervisor an anonymous note of complaint about the filing errors
    C. show the errors to the new assistant and tell him why they are errors in filing
    D. tell your supervisor that the new assistant makes a lot of errors in filing

---

KEY (CORRECT ANSWERS)

1. A
2. A
3. B
4. B
5. B

6. B
7. C
8. C
9. B
10. D

11. A
12. B
13. C
14. B
15. C

16. D
17. D
18. B
19. C
20. A

21. D
22. D
23. D
24. C

PHILOSOPHY, PRINCIPLES, PRACTICES, AND TECHNICS OF SUPERVISION, ADMINISTRATION, MANAGEMENT, AND ORGANIZATION

TABLE OF CONTENTS

	Page
MEANING OF SUPERVISION	1
THE OLD AND THE NEW SUPERVISION	1
THE EIGHT (8) BASIC PRINCIPLES OF THE NEW SUPERVISION	1
I. Principle of Responsibility	1
II. Principle of Authority	2
III. Principle of Self-Growth	2
IV. Principle of Individual Worth	2
V. Principle of Creative Leadership	2
VI. Principle of Success and Failure	2
VII. Principle of Science	3
VIII. Principle of Cooperation	3
WHAT IS ADMINISTRATION?	3
I. Practices Commonly Classed as "Supervisory"	3
II. Practices Commonly Classed as "Administrative"	3
III. Practices Commonly Classed as Both "Supervisory" and "Administrative"	4
RESPONSIBILITIES OF THE SUPERVISOR	4
COMPETENCIES OF THE SUPERVISOR	4
THE PROFESSIONAL SUPERVISOR-EMPLOYEE RELATIONSHIP	4
MINI-TEXT IN SUPERVISION, ADMINISTRATION, MANAGEMENT, AND ORGANIZATION	5
I. Brief Highlights	5
A. Levels of Management	6
B. What the Supervisor Must Learn	6
C. A Definition of Supervision	6
D. Elements of the Team Concept	6
E. Principles of Organization	6
F. The Four Important Parts of Every Job	7
G. Principles of Delegation	7
H. Principles of Effective Communications	7
I. Principles of Work Improvement	7
J. Areas of Job Improvement	7
K. Seven Key Points in Making Improvements	8

	L.	Corrective Techniques for Job Improvement	8
	M.	A Planning Checklist	8
	N.	Five Characteristics of Good Directions	9
	O.	Types of Directions	9
	P.	Controls	9
	Q.	Orienting the New Employee	9
	R.	Checklist for Orienting New Employees	9
	S.	Principles of Learning	10
	T.	Causes of Poor Performance	10
	U.	Four Major Steps in On-the-Job Instructions	10
	V.	Employees Want Five Things	10
	W.	Some Don'ts in Regard to Praise	11
	X.	How to Gain Your Workers' Confidence	11
	Y.	Sources of Employee Problems	11
	Z.	The Supervisor's Key to Discipline	11
	AA.	Five Important Processes of Management	12
	BB.	When the Supervisor Fails to Plan	12
	CC.	Fourteen General Principles of Management	12
	DD.	Change	12
II.	Brief Topical Summaries		13
	A.	Who/What is the Supervisor?	13
	B.	The Sociology of Work	13
	C.	Principles and Practices of Supervision	14
	D.	Dynamic Leadership	14
	E.	Processes for Solving Problems	15
	F.	Training for Results	15
	G.	Health, Safety, and Accident Prevention	16
	H.	Equal Employment Opportunity	16
	I.	Improving Communications	16
	J.	Self-Development	17
	K.	Teaching and Training	17
		1. The Teaching Process	17
		a. Preparation	17
		b. Presentation	18
		c. Summary	18
		d. Application	18
		e. Evaluation	18
		2. Teaching Methods	18
		a. Lecture	18
		b. Discussion	18
		c. Demonstration	19
		d. Performance	19
		e. Which Method to Use	19

PHILOSOPHY, PRINCIPLES, PRACTICES, AND TECHNICS OF SUPERVISION, ADMINISTRATION, MANAGEMENT, AND ORGANIZATION

MEANING OF SUPERVISION

The extension of the democratic philosophy has been accompanied by an extension in the scope of supervision. Modern leaders and supervisors no longer think of supervision in the narrow sense of being confined chiefly to visiting employees, supplying materials, or rating the staff. They regard supervision as being intimately related to all the concerned agencies of society, they speak of the supervisor's function in terms of "growth," rather than the "improvement" of employees.

This modern concept of supervision may be defined as follows: Supervision is leadership and the development of leadership within groups which are cooperatively engaged in inspection, research, training, guidance, and evaluation.

THE OLD AND THE NEW SUPERVISION

TRADITIONAL
1. Inspection
2. Focused on the employee
3. Visitation
4. Random and haphazard
5. Imposed and authoritarian
6. One person usually

MODERN
1. Study and analysis
2. Focused on aims, materials, methods, supervisors, employees, environment
3. Demonstrations, intervisitation, workshops, directed reading, bulletins, etc.
4. Definitely organized and planned (scientific)
5. Cooperative and democratic
6. Many persons involved (creative)

THE EIGHT (8) BASIC PRINCIPLES OF THE NEW SUPERVISION

I. Principle of Responsibility
   Authority to act and responsibility for acting must be joined.
   A. If you give responsibility, give authority.
   B. Define employee duties clearly.
   C. Protect employees from criticism by others.
   D. Recognize the rights as well as obligations of employees.
   E. Achieve the aims of a democratic society insofar as it is possible within the area of your work.
   F. Establish a situation favorable to training and learning.
   G. Accept ultimate responsibility for everything done in your section, unit, office, division, department.
   H. Good administration and good supervision are inseparable.

II. Principle of Authority
The success of the supervisor is measured by the extent to which the power of authority is not used.
   A. Exercise simplicity and informality in supervision
   B. Use the simplest machinery of supervision
   C. If it is good for the organization as a whole, it is probably justified.
   D. Seldom be arbitrary or authoritative.
   E. Do not base your work on the power of position or of personality.
   F. Permit and encourage the free expression of opinions.

III. Principle of Self-Growth
The success of the supervisor is measured by the extent to which, and the speed with which, he is no longer needed.
   A. Base criticism on principles, not on specifics.
   B. Point out higher activities to employees.
   C. Train for self-thinking by employees to meet new situations.
   D. Stimulate initiative, self-reliance, and individual responsibility
   E. Concentrate on stimulating the growth of employees rather than on removing defects.

IV. Principle of Individual Worth
Respect for the individual is a paramount consideration in supervision.
   A. Be human and sympathetic in dealing with employees.
   B. Don't nag about things to be done.
   C. Recognize the individual differences among employees and seek opportunities to permit best expression of each personality.

V. Principle of Creative Leadership
The best supervision is that which is not apparent to the employee.
   A. Stimulate, don't drive employees to creative action.
   B. Emphasize doing good things.
   C. Encourage employees to do what they do best.
   D. Do not be too greatly concerned with details of subject or method.
   E. Do not be concerned exclusively with immediate problems and activities.
   F. Reveal higher activities and make them both desired and maximally possible.
   G. Determine procedures in the light of each situation but see that these are derived from a sound basic philosophy.
   H. Aid, inspire, and lead so as to liberate the creative spirit latent in all good employees.

VI. Principle of Success and Failure
There are no unsuccessful employees, only unsuccessful supervisors who have failed to give proper leadership.
   A. Adapt suggestions to the capacities, attitudes, and prejudices of employees.
   B. Be gradual, be progressive, be persistent.
   C. Help the employee find the general principle; have the employee apply his own problem to the general principle.
   D. Give adequate appreciation for good work and honest effort.
   E. Anticipate employee difficulties and help to prevent them.
   F. Encourage employees to do the desirable things they will do anyway.
   G. Judge your supervision by the results it secures.

VII. Principle of Science
Successful supervision is scientific, objective, and experimental. It is based on facts, not on prejudices.
- A. Be cumulative in results.
- B. Never divorce your suggestions from the goals of training.
- C. Don't be impatient of results.
- D. Keep all matters on a professional, not a personal, level.
- E. Do not be concerned exclusively with immediate problems and activities.
- F. Use objective means of determining achievement and rating where possible.

VIII. Principle of Cooperation
Supervision is a cooperative enterprise between supervisor and employee.
- A. Begin with conditions as they are.
- B. Ask opinions of all involved when formulating policies.
- C. Organization is as good as its weakest link.
- D. Let employees help to determine policies and department programs.
- E. Be approachable and accessible—physically and mentally.
- F. Develop pleasant social relationships.

WHAT IS ADMINISTRATION

Administration is concerned with providing the environment, the material facilities, and the operational procedures that will promote the maximum growth and development of supervisors and employees. (Organization is an aspect and a concomitant of administration.)

There is no sharp line of demarcation between supervision and administration; these functions are intimately interrelated and, often, overlapping. They are complementary activities.

I. Practices Commonly Classed as "Supervisory"
- A. Conducting employees' conferences
- B. Visiting sections, units, offices, divisions, departments
- C. Arranging for demonstrations
- D. Examining plans
- E. Suggesting professional reading
- F. Interpreting bulletins
- G. Recommending in-service training courses
- H. Encouraging experimentation
- I. Appraising employee morale
- J. Providing for intervisitation

II. Practices Commonly Classified as "Administrative"
- A. Management of the office
- B. Arrangement of schedules for extra duties
- C. Assignment of rooms or areas
- D. Distribution of supplies
- E. Keeping records and reports
- F. Care of audio-visual materials
- G. Keeping inventory records
- H. Checking record cards and books

I. Programming special activities
J. Checking on the attendance and punctuality of employees

III. Practices Commonly Classified as Both "Supervisory" and "Administrative"
   A. Program construction
   B. Testing or evaluating outcomes
   C. Personnel accounting
   D. Ordering instructional materials

RESPONSIBILITIES OF THE SUPERVISOR

A person employed in a supervisory capacity must constantly be able to improve his own efficiency and ability. He represent the employer to the employees and only continuous self-examination can make him a capable supervisor.

Leadership and training are the supervisor's responsibility. An efficient working unit is one in which the employees work with the supervisor. It is his job to bring out the best in his employees. He must always be relaxed, courteous, and calm in his association with his employees. Their feelings are important, and a harsh attitude does not develop the most efficient employees.

COMPETENCES OF THE SUPERVISOR

I. Complete knowledge of the duties and responsibilities of his position.
II. To be able to organize a job, plan ahead, and carry through.
III. To have self-confidence and initiative.
IV. To be able to handle the unexpected situation and make quick decisions.
V. To be able to properly train subordinates in the positions they are best suited for.
VI. To be able to keep good human relations among his subordinates.
VII. To be able to keep good human relations between his subordinates and himself and to earn their respect and trust.

THE PROFESSIONAL SUPERVISOR-EMPLOYEE RELATIONSHIP

There are two kinds of efficiency: one kind is only apparent and is produced in organizations through the exercise of mere discipline; this is but a simulation of the second, or true, efficiency which springs from spontaneous cooperation. If you are a manager, no matter how great or small your responsibility, it is your job, in the final analysis, to create and develop this involuntary cooperation among the people whom you supervise. For, no matter how powerful a combination of money, machines, and materials a company may have, this is a dead and sterile thing without a team of willing, thinking, and articulate people to guide it.

The following 21 points are presented as indicative of the exemplary basic relationship that should exist between supervisor and employee:

1. Each person wants to be liked and respected by his fellow employee and wants to be treated with consideration and respect by his superior.
2. The most competent employee will make an error. However, in a unit where good relations exist between the supervisor and his employees, tenseness and fear do not exist. Thus, errors are not hidden or covered up, and the efficiency of a unit is not impaired.

3. Subordinates resent rules, regulations, or orders that are unreasonable or unexplained.
4. Subordinates are quick to resent unfairness, harshness, injustices, and favoritism.
5. An employee will accept responsibility if he knows that he will be complimented for a job well done, and not too harshly chastised for failure; that his supervisor will check the cause of the failure, and, if it was the supervisor's fault, he will assume the blame therefore. If it was the employee's fault, his supervisor will explain the correct method or means of handling the responsibility.
6. An employee wants to receive credit for a suggestion he has made, that is used. If a suggestion cannot be used, the employee is entitled to an explanation. The supervisor should not say "no" and close the subject.
7. Fear and worry slow up a worker's ability. Poor working environment can impair his physical and mental health. A good supervisor avoids forceful methods, threats, and arguments to get a job done.
8. A forceful supervisor is able to train his employees individually and as a team, and is able to motivate them in the proper channels.
9. A mature supervisor is able to properly evaluate his subordinates and to keep them happy and satisfied.
10. A sensitive supervisor will never patronize his subordinates.
11. A worthy supervisor will respect his employees' confidences.
12. Definite and clear-cut responsibilities should be assigned to each executive.
13. Responsibility should always be coupled with corresponding authority.
14. No change should be made in the scope or responsibilities of a position without a definite understanding to that effect on the part of all persons concerned.
15. No executive or employee, occupying a single position in the organization, should be subject to definite orders from more than one source.
16. Orders should never be given to subordinates over the head of a responsible executive. Rather than do this, the officer in question should be supplanted.
17. Criticisms of subordinates should, whoever possible, be made privately, and in no case should a subordinate be criticized in the presence of executives or employees of equal or lower rank.
18. No dispute or difference between executives or employees as to authority or responsibilities should be considered too trivial for prompt and careful adjudication.
19. Promotions, wage changes, and disciplinary action should always be approved by the executive immediately superior to the one directly responsible.
20. No executive or employee should ever be required, or expected, to be at the same time an assistant to, and critic of, another.
21. Any executive whose work is subject to regular inspection should, wherever practicable, be given the assistance and facilities necessary to enable him to maintain an independent check of the quality of his work.

MINI-TEXT IN SUPERVISION, ADMINISTRATION, MANAGEMENT, AND ORGANIZATION

I. Brief Highlights

Listed concisely and sequentially are major headings and important data in the field for quick recall and review.

A. Levels of Management
Any organization of some size has several levels of management. In terms of a ladder, the levels are:

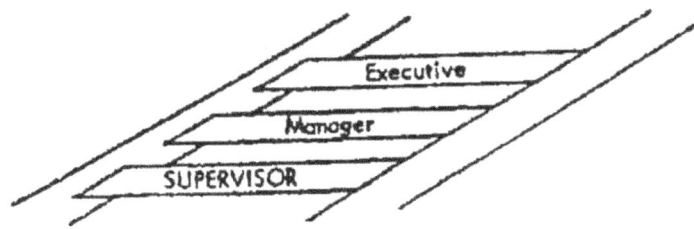

The first level is very important because it is the beginning point of management leadership.

B. What the Supervisor Must Learn
A supervisor must learn to:
1. Deal with people and their differences
2. Get the job done through people
3. Recognize the problems when they exist
4. Overcome obstacles to good performance
5. Evaluate the performance of people
6. Check his own performance in terms of accomplishment

C. A Definition of Supervisor
The term supervisor means any individual having authority, in the interests of the employer, to hire, transfer, suspend, lay-off, recall, promote, discharge, assign, reward, or discipline other employees or responsibility to direct them, or to adjust their grievances, or effectively to recommend such action, if, in connection with the foregoing, exercise of such authority is not of a merely routine or clerical nature but requires the use of independent judgment.

D. Elements of the Team Concept
What is involved in teamwork? The component parts are:
1. Members
2. A leader
3. Goals
4. Plans
5. Cooperation
6. Spirit

E. Principles of Organization
1. A team member must know what his job is.
2. Be sure that the nature and scope of a job are understood.
3. Authority and responsibility should be carefully spelled out.
4. A supervisor should be permitted to make the maximum number of decisions affecting his employees.
5. Employees should report to only one supervisor.
6. A supervisor should direct only as many employees as he can handle effectively.
7. An organization plan should be flexible.

8. Inspection and performance of work should be separate.
9. Organizational problems should receive immediate attention.
10. Assign work in line with ability and experience.

F. The Four Important Parts of Every Job
1. Inherent in every job is the *accountability* for results.
2. A second set of factors in every job is *responsibilities*.
3. Along with duties and responsibilities one must have the *authority* to act within certain limits without obtaining permission to proceed.
4. No job exists in a vacuum. The supervisor is surrounded by key *relationships*.

G. Principles of Delegation
Where work is delegated for the first time, the supervisor should think in terms of these questions:
1. Who is best qualified to do this?
2. Can an employee improve his abilities by doing this?
3. How long should an employee spend on this?
4. Are there any special problems for which he will need guidance?
5. How broad a delegation can I make?

H. Principles of Effective Communications
1. Determine the media.
2. To whom directed?
3. Identification and source authority.
4. Is communication understood?

I. Principles of Work Improvement
1. Most people usually do only the work which is assigned to them.
2. Workers are likely to fit assigned work into the time available to perform it.
3. A good workload usually stimulates output.
4. People usually do their best work when they know that results will be reviewed or inspected.
5. Employees usually feel that someone else is responsible for conditions of work, workplace layout, job methods, type of tools/equipment, and other such factors.
6. Employees are usually defensive about their job security.
7. Employees have natural resistance to change.
8. Employees can support or destroy a supervisor.
9. A supervisor usually earns the respect of his people through his personal example of diligence and efficiency.

J. Areas of Job Improvement
The areas of job improvement are quite numerous, but the most common ones which a supervisor can identify and utilize are:
1. Departmental layout
2. Flow of work
3. Workplace layout
4. Utilization of manpower
5. Work methods
6. Materials handling

7. Utilization
8. Motion economy

K. Seven Key Points in Making Improvements
1. Select the job to be improved
2. Study how it is being done now
3. Question the present method
4. Determine actions to be taken
5. Chart proposed method
6. Get approval and apply
7. Solicit worker participation

l. Corrective Techniques of Job Improvement
Specific Problems
1. Size of workload
2. Inability to meet schedules
3. Strain and fatigue
4. Improper use of men and skills
5. Waste, poor quality, unsafe conditions
6. Bottleneck conditions that hinder output
7. Poor utilization of equipment and machine
8. Efficiency and productivity of labor

General Improvement
1. Departmental layout
2. Flow of work
3. Work plan layout
4. Utilization of manpower
5. Work methods
6. Materials handling
7. Utilization of equipment
8. Motion economy

Corrective Techniques
1. Study with scale model
2. Flow chart study
3. Motion analysis
4. Comparison of units produced to standard allowance
5. Methods analysis
6. Flow chart and equipment study
7. Down time vs. running time
8. Motion analysis

M. A Planning Checklist
1. Objectives
2. Controls
3. Delegations
4. Communications
5. Resources
6. Manpower

7. Equipment
8. Supplies and materials
9. Utilization of time
10. Safety
11. Money
12. Work
13. Timing of improvements

N. Five Characteristics of Good Directions
In order to get results, directions must be:
1. Possible of accomplishment
2. Agreeable with worker interests
3. Related to mission
4. Planned and complete
5. Unmistakably clear

O. Types of Directions
1. Demands or direct orders
2. Requests
3. Suggestion or implication
4. volunteering

P. Controls
A typical listing of the overall areas in which the supervisor should establish controls might be:
1. Manpower
2. Materials
3. Quality of work
4. Quantity of work
5. Time
6. Space
7. Money
8. Methods

Q. Orienting the New Employee
1. Prepare for him
2. Welcome the new employee
3. Orientation for the job
4. Follow-up

R. Checklist for Orienting New Employees   Yes   No
1. Do you appreciate the feelings of new employees
   when they first report for work?   ___   ___
2. Are you aware of the fact that the new employee must
   make a big adjustment to his job?   ___   ___
3. Have you given him good reasons for liking the job and
   the organization?   ___   ___
4. Have you prepared for his first day on the job?   ___   ___
5. Did you welcome him cordially and make him feel needed?   ___   ___

	Yes	No

6. Did you establish rapport with him so that he feels free to talk and discuss matters with you? ___ ___
7. Did you explain his job to him and his relationship to you? ___ ___
8. Does he know that his work will be evaluated periodically on a basis that is fair and objective? ___ ___
9. Did you introduce him to his fellow workers in such a way that they are likely to accept him? ___ ___
10. Does he know what employee benefits he will receive? ___ ___
11. Does he understand the importance of being on the job and what to do if he must leave his duty station? ___ ___
12. Has he been impressed with the importance of accident prevention and safe practice? ___ ___
13. Does he generally know his way around the department? ___ ___
14. Is he under the guidance of a sponsor who will teach the right way of doing things? ___ ___
15. Do you plan to follow-up so that he will continue to adjust successfully to his job? ___ ___

S. Principles of Learning
1. Motivation
2. Demonstration or explanation
3. Practice

T. Causes of Poor Performance
1. Improper training for job
2. Wrong tools
3. Inadequate directions
4. Lack of supervisory follow-up
5. Poor communications
6. Lack of standards of performance
7. Wrong work habits
8. Low morale
9. Other

U. Four Major Steps in On-The-Job Instruction
1. Prepare the worker
2. Present the operation
3. Tryout performance
4. Follow-up

V. Employees Want Five Things
1. Security
2. Opportunity
3. Recognition
4. Inclusion
5. Expression

W. Some Don'ts in Regard to Praise
1. Don't praise a person for something he hasn't done.
2. Don't praise a person unless you can be sincere.
3. Don't be sparing in praise just because your superior withholds it from you.
4. Don't let too much time elapse between good performance and recognition of it

X. How to Gain Your Workers' Confidence
Methods of developing confidence include such things as:
1. Knowing the interests, habits, hobbies of employees
2. Admitting your own inadequacies
3. Sharing and telling of confidence in others
4. Supporting people when they are in trouble
5. Delegating matters that can be well handled
6. Being frank and straightforward about problems and working conditions
7. Encouraging others to bring their problems to you
8. Taking action on problems which impede worker progress

Y. Sources of Employee Problems
On-the-job causes might be such things as:
1. A feeling that favoritism is exercised in assignments
2. Assignment of overtime
3. An undue amount of supervision
4. Changing methods or systems
5. Stealing of ideas or trade secrets
6. Lack of interest in job
7. Threat of reduction in force
8. Ignorance or lack of communications
9. Poor equipment
10. Lack of knowing how supervisor feels toward employee
11. Shift assignments

Off-the-job problems might have to do with:
1. Health
2. Finances
3. Housing
4. Family

Z. The Supervisor's Key to Discipline
There are several key points about discipline which the supervisor should keep in mind:
1. Job discipline is one of the disciplines of life and is directed by the supervisor.
2. It is more important to correct an employee fault than to fix blame for it.
3. Employee performance is affected by problems both on the job and off.
4. Sudden or abrupt changes in behavior can be indications of important employee problems.
5. Problems should be dealt with as soon as possible after they are identified.
6. The attitude of the supervisor may have more to do with solving problems than the techniques of problem solving.
7. Correction of employee behavior should be resorted to only after the supervisor is sure that training or counseling will not be helpful.

8. Be sure to document your disciplinary actions.
9. Make sure that you are disciplining on the basis of facts rather than personal feelings.
10. Take each disciplinary step in order, being careful not to make snap judgments, or decisions based on impatience.

AA. Five Important Processes of Management
1. Planning
2. Organizing
3. Scheduling
4. Controlling
5. Motivating

BB. When the Supervisor Fails to Plan
1. Supervisor creates impression of not knowing his job
2. May lead to excessive overtime
3. Job runs itself—supervisor lacks control
4. Deadlines and appointments missed
5. Parts of the work go undone
6. Work interrupted by emergencies
7. Sets a bad example
8. Uneven workload creates peaks and valleys
9. Too much time on minor details at expense of more important tasks

CC. Fourteen General Principles of Management
1. Division of work
2. Authority and responsibility
3. Discipline
4. Unity of command
5. Unity of direction
6. Subordination of individual interest to general interest
7. Remuneration of personnel
8. Centralization
9. Scalar chain
10. Order
11. Equity
12. Stability of tenure of personnel
13. Initiative
14. Esprit de corps

DD. Change

Bringing about change is perhaps attempted more often, and yet less well understood, than anything else the supervisor does. How do people generally react to change? (People tend to resist change that is imposed upon them by other individuals or circumstances.

Change is characteristic of every situation. It is a part of every real endeavor where the efforts of people are concerned.

1. Why do people resist change?
   People may resist change because of:
   a. Fear of the unknown
   b. Implied criticism
   c. Unpleasant experiences in the past
   d. Fear of loss of status
   e. Threat to the ego
   f. Fear of loss of economic stability

2. How can we best overcome the resistance to change?
   In initiating change, take these steps:
   a. Get ready to sell
   b. Identify sources of help
   c. Anticipate objections
   d. Sell benefits
   e. Listen in depth
   f. Follow up

II. Brief Topical Summaries

   A. Who/What is the Supervisor?
      1. The supervisor is often called the "highest level employee and the lowest level manager."
      2. A supervisor is a member of both management and the work group. He acts as a bridge between the two.
      3. Most problems in supervision are in the area of human relations, or people problems.
      4. Employees expect: Respect, opportunity to learn and to advance, and a sense of belonging, and so forth.
      5. Supervisors are responsible for directing people and organizing work. Planning is of paramount importance.
      6. A position description is a set of duties and responsibilities inherent to a given position.
      7. It is important to keep the position description up-to-date and to provide each employee with his own copy.

   B. The Sociology of Work
      1. People are alike in many ways; however, each individual is unique.
      2. The supervisor is challenged in getting to know employee differences. Acquiring skills in evaluating individuals is an asset.
      3. Maintaining meaningful working relationships in the organization is of great importance.
      4. The supervisor has an obligation to help individuals to develop to their fullest potential.
      5. Job rotation on a planned basis helps to build versatility and to maintain interest and enthusiasm in work groups.
      6. Cross training (job rotation) provides backup skills.

7. The supervisor can help reduce tension by maintaining a sense of humor, providing guidance to employees, and by making reasonable and timely decisions. Employees respond favorably to working under reasonably predictable circumstances.
8. Change is characteristic of all managerial behavior. The supervisor must adjust to changes in procedures, new methods, technological changes, and to a number of new and sometimes challenging situations.
9. To overcome the natural tendency for people to resist change, the supervisor should become more skillful in initiating change.

C. Principles and Practices of Supervision
1. Employees should be required to answer to only one superior.
2. A supervisor can effectively direct only a limited number of employees, depending upon the complexity, variety, and proximity of the jobs involved.
3. The organizational chart presents the organization in graphic form. It reflects lines of authority and responsibility as well as interrelationships of units within the organization.
4. Distribution of work can be improved through an analysis using the "Work Distribution Chart."
5. The "Work Distribution Chart" reflects the division of work within a unit in understandable form.
6. When related tasks are given to an employee, he has a better chance of increasing his skills through training.
7. The individual who is given the responsibility for tasks must also be given the appropriate authority to insure adequate results.
8. The supervisor should delegate repetitive, routine work. Preparation of recurring reports, maintaining leave and attendance records are some examples.
9. Good discipline is essential to good task performance. Discipline is reflected in the actions of employees on the job in the absence of supervision.
10. Disciplinary action may have to be taken when the positive aspects of discipline have failed. Reprimand, warning, and suspension are examples of disciplinary action.
11. If a situation calls for a reprimand, be sure it is deserved and remember it is to be done in private.

D. Dynamic Leadership
1. A style is a personal method or manner of exerting influence.
2. Authoritarian leaders often see themselves as the source of power and authority.
3. The democratic leader often perceives the group as the source of authority and power.
4. Supervisors tend to do better when using the pattern of leadership that is most natural for them.
5. Social scientists suggest that the effective supervisor use the leadership style that best fits the problem or circumstances involved.
6. All four styles—telling, selling, consulting, joining—have their place. Using one does not preclude using the other at another time.

7. The theory X point of view assumes that the average person dislikes work, will avoid it whenever possible, and must be coerced to achieve organizational objectives.
8. The theory Y point of view assumes that the average person considers work to be a natural as play, and, when the individual is committed, he requires little supervision or direction to accomplish desired objectives.
9. The leader's basic assumptions concerning human behavior and human nature affect his actions, decisions, and other managerial practices.
10. Dissatisfaction among employees is often present, but difficult to isolate. The supervisor should seek to weaken dissatisfaction by keeping promises, being sincere and considerate, keeping employees informed, and so forth.
11. Constructive suggestions should be encouraged during the natural progress of the work.

E. Processes for Solving Problems
1. People find their daily tasks more meaningful and satisfying when they can improve them.
2. The causes of problems, or the key factors, are often hidden in the background. Ability to solve problems often involves the ability to isolate them from their backgrounds. There is some substance to the cliché that some persons "can't see the forest for the trees."
3. New procedures are often developed from old ones. Problems should be broken down into manageable parts. New ideas can be adapted from old one.
4. People think differently in problem-solving situations. Using a logical, patterned approach is often useful. One approach found to be useful includes these steps:
   a. Define the problem
   b. Establish objectives
   c. Get the facts
   d. Weigh and decide
   e. Take action
   f. Evaluate action

F. Training for Results
1. Participants respond best when they feel training is important to them.
2. The supervisor has responsibility for the training and development of those who report to him.
3. When training is delegated to others, great care must be exercised to insure the trainer has knowledge, aptitude, and interest for his work as a trainer.
4. Training (learning) of some type goes on continually. The most successful supervisor makes certain the learning contributes in a productive manner to operational goals.
5. New employees are particularly susceptible to training. Older employees facing new job situations require specific training, as well as having need for development and growth opportunities.
6. Training needs require continuous monitoring.
7. The training officer of an agency is a professional with a responsibility to assist supervisors in solving training problems.

8. Many of the self-development steps important to the supervisor's own growth are equally important to the development of peers and subordinates. Knowledge of these is important when the supervisor consults with others on development and growth opportunities.

G. Health, Safety, and Accident Prevention
1. Management-minded supervisors take appropriate measures to assist employees in maintaining health and in assuring safe practices in the work environment.
2. Effective safety training and practices help to avoid injury and accidents.
3. Safety should be a management goal. All infractions of safety which are observed should be corrected without exception.
4. Employees' safety attitude, training and instruction, provision of safe tools and equipment, supervision, and leadership are considered highly important factors which contribute to safety and which can be influenced directly by supervisors.
5. When accidents do occur, they should be investigated promptly for very important reasons, including the fact that information which is gained can be used to prevent accidents in the future.

H. Equal Employment Opportunity
1. The supervisor should endeavor to treat all employees fairly, without regard to religion, race, sex, or national origin.
2. Groups tend to reflect the attitude of the leader. Prejudice can be detected even in very subtle form. Supervisors must strive to create a feeling of mutual respect and confidence in every employee.
3. Complete utilization of all human resources is a national goal. Equitable consideration should be accorded women in the work force, minority-group members, the physically and mentally handicapped, and the older employee. The important question is: "Who can do the job?"
4. Training opportunities, recognition for performance, overtime assignments, promotional opportunities, and all other personnel actions are to be handled on an equitable basis.

I. Improving Communications
1. Communications is achieving understanding between the sender and the receiver of a message. It also means sharing information—the creation of understanding.
2. Communication is basic to all human activity. Words are means of conveying meanings; however, real meanings are in people.
3. There are very practical differences in the effectiveness of one-way, impersonal, and two-way communications. Words spoken face-to-face are better understood. Telephone conversations are effective, but lack the rapport of person-to-person exchanges. The whole person communicates.
4. Cooperation and communication in an organization go hand in hand. When there is a mutual respect between people, spelling out rules and procedures for communicating is unnecessary.
5. There are several barriers to effective communications. These include failure to listen with respect and understanding, lack of skill in feedback, and misinterpreting the meanings of words used by the speaker. It is also common

practice to listen to what we want to hear, and tune out things we do not want to hear.
6. Communication is management's chief problem. The supervisor should accept the challenge to communicate more effectively and to improve interagency and intra-agency communications.
7. The supervisor may often plan for and conduct meetings. The planning phase is critical and may determine the success or the failure of a meeting.
8. Speaking before groups usually requires extra effort. Stage fright may never disappear completely, but it can be controlled.

J. Self-Development
1. Every employee is responsible for his own self-development.
2. Toastmaster and toastmistress clubs offer opportunities to improve skills in oral communications.
3. Planning for one's own self-development is of vital importance. Supervisors know their own strengths and limitations better than anyone else.
4. Many opportunities are open to aid the supervisor in his developmental efforts, including job assignments; training opportunities, both governmental and non-governmental—to include universities and professional conferences and seminars.
5. Programmed instruction offers a means of studying at one's own rate.
6. Where difficulties may arise from a supervisor's being away from his work for training, he may participate in televised home study or correspondence courses to meet his self-development needs.

K. Teaching and Training
1. The Teaching Process
Teaching is encouraging and guiding the learning activities of students toward established goals. In most cases this process consists of five steps: preparation, presentation, summarization, evaluation, and application.

   a. Preparation
   Preparation is two-fold in nature; that of the supervisor and the employee. Preparation by the supervisor is absolutely essential to success. He must know what, when, where, how, and whom he will teach. Some of the factors that should be considered are:
   1) The objectives
   2) The materials needed
   3) The methods to be used
   4) Employee participation
   5) Employee interest
   6) Training aids
   7) Evaluation
   8) Summarization

   Employee preparation consists in preparing the employee to receive the material. Probably the most important single factor in the preparation of the employee is arousing and maintaining his interest. He must know the objectives of the training, why he is there, how the material can be used, and its importance to him.

b. Presentation
In presentation, have a carefully designed plan and follow it. The plan should be accurate and complete, yet flexible enough to meet situations as they arise. The method of presentation will be determined by the particular situation and objectives.

c. Summary
A summary should be made at the end of every training unit and program. In addition, there may be internal summaries depending on the nature of the material being taught. The important thing is that the trainee must always be able to understand how each part of the new material relates to the whole.

d. Application
The supervisor must arrange work so the employee will be given a chance to apply new knowledge or skills while the material is still clear in his mind and interest is high. The trainee does not really know whether he has learned the material until he has been given a chance to apply it. If the material is not applied, it loses most of its value.

e. Evaluation
The purpose of all training is to promote learning. To determine whether the training has been a success or failure, the supervisor must evaluate this learning.
In the broadest sense, evaluation includes all the devices, methods, skills, and techniques used by the supervisor to keep himself and the employees informed as to their progress toward the objectives they are pursuing. The extent to which the employee has mastered the knowledge, skills, and abilities, or changed his attitudes, as determined by the program objectives, is the extent to which instruction has succeeded or failed.
Evaluation should not be confined to the end of the lesson, day, or program but should be used continuously. We shall note later the way this relates to the rest of the teaching process.

2. Teaching Methods
A teaching method is a pattern of identifiable student and instructor activity used in presenting training material.
All supervisors are faced with the problem of deciding which method should be used at a given time.

a. Lecture
The lecture is direct oral presentation of material by the supervisor. The present trend is to place less emphasis on the trainer's activity and more on that of the trainee.

b. Discussion
Teaching by discussion or conference involves using questions and other techniques to arouse interest and focus attention upon certain areas, and by doing so creating a learning situation. This can be one of the most

valuable methods because it gives the employees an opportunity to express their ideas and pool their knowledge.

    c. Demonstration
The demonstration is used to teach how something works or how to do something. It can be used to show a principle or what the results of a series of actions will be. A well-staged demonstration is particularly effective because it shows proper methods of performance in a realistic manner.

    d. Performance
Performance is one of the most fundamental of all learning techniques or teaching methods. The trainee may be able to tell how a specific operation should be performed but he cannot be sure he knows how to perform the operation until he has done so.
As with all methods, there are certain advantages and disadvantages to each method.

    e. Which Method to Use
Moreover, there are other methods and techniques of teaching. It is difficult to use any method without other methods entering into it. In any learning situation, a combination of methods is usually more effective than any one method alone.

Finally, evaluation must be integrated into the other aspects of the teaching-learning process.

It must be used in the motivation of the trainees; it must be used to assist in developing understanding during the training; and it must be related to employee application of the results of training.

This is distinctly the role of the supervisor.

www.ingramcontent.com/pod-product-compliance
Lightning Source LLC
Chambersburg PA
CBHW081826300426
44116CB00014B/2503